Perfecting & Reforming
PERSONAL DEVOTION

Linwood Jackson, Jr.

PUBLISHED BY FIDELI PUBLISHING, INC.

ISBN: 978-1-970730-88-3 (hardcover)
          978-1-970730-87-6 (paperback)

For information, email the author at
LinwoodJackson@hotmail.com

Published by
Fideli Publishing, Inc.
www.FideliPublishing.com

Contents

Introduction

1. To profess faith in the Bible's philosophy is to embark on a journey that demands knowing the *voice* behind its understanding, no matter how faint or fervent that faith may be. The Mind guiding Scripture calls us to "seek ye out of the book of the LORD, and read" (Isaiah 34:16), urging every heart to explore the Bible's character without restraint. The willing mind should fall before the throne of the Bible's wisdom, seeking re-education in worship and in service (Philippians 3:8). To be "so vexed" that one's soul aches for its knowledge is no weakness; it's a rare longing that is met with the promise: "Blessed are they that mourn: for they shall be comforted" (2 Samuel 13:2, Matthew 5:4). Those who hunger for right understanding will be filled, their thirst quenched by fact (Matthew 5:6).

2. The devotional conversation's soul must not bow to the clamor of its heart. The spirit of its mind, meant to govern, should not serve its heart's unruly spiritual passions (Ephesians 2:3). Born without pure knowledge, it naturally chases strange religious desires, but the Bible's words awaken a deeper yearning (Judges 13:25). Moved by its touch, the heart of our belief turns from its natural human and religious bent, purifying itself through faith (Acts 15:9). This is no mere instinct, it's a unique stirring, even a call to reject what is against religious nature to embrace the Bible's life-giving truth (Romans 1:26).

3. The faithful feel this pull: "The spirit within me constraineth me" (Job 32:18), they say. The Bible's counsel

gives life, quickening the inward parts of the belief's *body*, while that *body* ultimately offers nothing but spiritual death (2 Corinthians 3:6, John 6:63). To live by the spirit within the body of the belief is to die by a restricted understanding, but through the Bible's words we mortify its deeds and find a refreshed experience (Romans 8:13). The heart's strange appetites—whether inherited or cultivated—must yield to reason and a sanctified faith. Only a mind renewed by the counsel of the scripture's Mind can govern the heart, cleansing the conversation from a religion of false appearance (2 Corinthians 5:12).

4. A faith rooted in tradition or superstition keeps the conversation asleep, its temple defiled by self-cultivated creeds (Ephesians 2:3). The Bible stirs the mind to reclaim its authority, seeking the source of its intended prompting (Acts 3:19). To ignore this call is to embrace spiritual decay, to love the death of the intellect over a living heart (Proverbs 8:36). But when the heart seeks the Bible's praise, studying its voice with diligence, it finds health; its words are "life unto those that find them, and health to all their flesh" (Proverbs 4:22). This is the soul's renewal, a restoration of the mind to house Bible truth, proving what is excellent and nourishing to the natural and to the devotional character (Philippians 1:10,11).

5. Only the spirit of the mind, reborn through faith, can enter into the present and already existing *kingdom* of *God*. (1 Corinthians 5:5). Without reformation now, how will a heart bound by fear or unbelief find peace in that *experience*? The time is now to "acquaint thyself with him, and be at peace" (Job 22:21). The law of the Bible's philosophy must not be forgotten; the heart must keep its commandments, inclining to wisdom and understanding (Proverbs 3:1, 2:2; 5:1,2, 2:10,11).

6. Through obedience to that philosophy, the Bible's words delivers captives of religion, restores sight to the spiritually maimed, and sets the bruised devotional conversation free (Luke 4:18). "Do not forget my law," it urges, for our love towards it is shown in keeping its counsel (Proverbs 3:1, John 14:15). The living God's chief apostle magnified this law, making it honorable, even dying for it (Isaiah 42:21, 51:4). By this law of understanding we become lights of the intended devotional experience (Romans 8:2, 2 Corinthians 5:21). This is the believer's task: to seek the Bible's will, to know its thoughts through obedience, searching its fact through its words (Galatians 6:2, Ecclesiastes 7:25, Zechariah 7:12).

7. Its *kingdom* offers "all spiritual blessings" through faith, a flood of wisdom and revelation for refreshing our personal and devotional character (Ephesians 1:3, Colossians 1:9). The heart, left to itself, wallows in mud, its thoughts clouded by intemperance (Ecclesiastes 1:8). Only the wisdom found within living God's chief apostle's sacrifice; his suffering on the tree and the guiding mediation of that allegory; frees us from this bondage (Psalm 50:23). This revelation invites us to "handle" the body of that man's belief, to prove its commandments by faith, ordering our lives aright (Luke 24:39; Proverbs 19:24, 12:11, Titus 2:11).

8. This wisdom, found in the conversation of the living God's chief apostle, is the promise of life, the Bible's power to overcome sin (religious error) (2 Timothy 2:1, 1 John 5:12). Where sin (spiritual negligence) abounds, grace overflows, making us followers of a renewed state of mind (Romans 5:20, 6:18). The Bible's ordinances, rooted in justice, strengthen the mind to act against impure spiritual desires (Isaiah 58:2, 1 Peter 1:13). Wisdom, gained through obedience to the Bible's words, becomes a shield, fortifying

the soul against the heart's inclinations (Ecclesiastes 7:19, 7:12).

9. No human heart can satisfy its own longing; only the guidance given through the Bible's *voice* can fill it (Ecclesiastes 1:8). Through the mediation of the living God's chief apostle's example, the mind gains strength to govern, distributing its wealth to those in need (Luke 18:22). To know the Bible is to prove its truth, to let its countenance shine through a life transformed (1 Chronicles 28:9). This is why the prophet Jeremiah counsels us to seek this understanding with all of our heart, to the end that we may find the peace that rightly perfects and reforms our personal devotion into a living testimony. (Jeremiah 29:13).

1

Practical Living
Through Self-Regulation

1. When meditating on the depth of the Bible's philosophy, one finds it to be far more than a set of beliefs or rituals passed down through generations. Instead, a vibrant philosophical culture, interwoven within a narrative of allegorical and figurative images, emerges to display the "righteousness" of the Bible. This righteousness is an intended kindness or benevolence for the devotional conversation's character. Obtaining this experience is not a passive endeavor; it requires consistently exercising what is learned from the Bible.

2. The Bible's discipline, as exemplified by the minds within it, serves as a guiding light for its students. One will find the Bible counseling on the correct devotional nature, encouraging us to let our belief try out its knowledge for guidance. Yet, this transformation cannot occur in isolation from the corrupting influences of the religious world. While it is true that we have to be in the religious world and not of

the religious world, only by making sense of and breaking free from the shackles of religious desires can one fully embrace the knowledge that leads to communion with the Bible. Without this fundamental shift in perspective, the gift of the intended devotional nature remains elusive, leaving one adrift in a sea of spiritual stagnation.

3. "Eternal life," far from being a distant promise, emerges as a present reality for those who seek the wisdom of the Bible's character. This wisdom, embodied within the conversation of the living God's chief apostle, offers liberation from the bondage of personal and devotional error. It is a costly knowledge, demanding nothing less than total surrender and sacrifice of self. Through this knowledge, the Bible's students are invited into a deeper intimacy with it, where every aspect of their being is transformed by its *grace*. It is through faith in its *name* that one appropriates its promises, strengthening a right devotional life within the living experience.

4. True faith, grounded in the wisdom of the Bible's character, is a precious gift bestowed upon the repentant conversation. It is not achieved through human effort or merit but is acquired through a journey of obedience and self-renunciation. The true devotional reformer does not seek religious accolades but the *praise* of understanding. Their faith is not a mere intellectual assent but a heartfelt commitment to the principle and definition of salvation, leading to a profound love for the Bible, and a desire to live within its counsel.

5. The path to grace requires a radical departure from the prevailing spirit within the religious world and a wholehearted embrace of creation's *High Priest*. This transformation is a conscious choice to forsake the culture of the religious world to embrace the transformative power of *grace*.

Only through this shift in perspective can one truly experience the fullness of the intended redemption to become a vessel of purpose.

6. When the conversation is united with the Bible's philosophy, their devotional life is no longer their own, but hidden within that science and discipline. It no longer lives for its self but for the living God's will, abiding in the love of that will through growing familiar with that will's counsel. If ensnared by the spirit of the religious world, love for this understanding will not be accepted or acceptable. True love for the Bible is manifested through willingness to know its character, which character our conversation is called to emulate through faithful adherence to its *Mind*.

7. The allegory concerning the incarnation signifies the fulfillment of the Bible's character within the devotional conversation. The sacrifice of the living God's chief apostle is an example of necessary liberation from philosophies and traditions within the religious world, attaining sobriety and intelligence through the statement of his sacrificed body; this is why it says, "Christ hath redeemed us from the law."[1] This transformation demands a separation from the mindset of the religious world and a consecration of heart and mind to a service for the personal religion. By perfecting the likeness of this man's statement within, we are to cleanse our belief from religious error, attaining a right spiritual understanding for an intended devotional experience.

8. The promises of the living God are not empty words but are living truths given to cleanse the innermost being. The intended devotional experience will engrave truth in the inward parts,[2] and the law or principle of the living God's benevolence serves as the standard of truth. To exist within

---

1   Galatians 3:13
2   Psalm 51:6

this principle's presence, conversations must allow its mindset to increase within them. The character of the Bible's philosophy is imparted through the sanctification of the conversation, enabling it to build a spiritual dwelling fit for holding a unique piece of the living God's *Mind*. As they strive for perfection, conversations are polished into the likeness of a palace,[3] reflecting the glory of the heavenly Jerusalem, which is the institution of their training.

9. The soul temple must endure the refining fire of suffering a separation from self-cultivated and inherited religious belief if it is to bear a likeness to the living God's character. By embracing the work of faith with power,[4] they conform to the image of Christ, reflecting His moral image in every aspect of their lives. Through the knowledge of God and Jesus our Lord, believers obtain wisdom for life and godliness, resisting the allure of legalistic religion and destructive lusts. Liberated from sin, they become servants of God, destined for holiness and everlasting life through the transformative power of His grace.

---

3   Psalm 144:12
4   2 Thessalonians 1:11

2

As Alive From The Flesh

1. When examining, as it is within the New Testament, the apostles' philosophy, we are drawn into a spiritual journey that transcends mere doctrine or ritual. This *faith* is deeply rooted in the righteousness or kindness of the living God's *character* and manifests through unwavering adherence to that character's will and wisdom. The labor of the living God's chief apostle stands at the heart of this faith, which is accessed through an intimate knowledge of that labor's intention. This journey requires spiritual growth and revelation, a dynamic process of growth and development leading the devotional conversation towards communion with the Bible.

2. The Bible's philosophy exemplifies a path for modern believers, emphasizing the necessity of the devotional conversation's growth and development through understanding. This transformation is possible only by removing one's mind from the religious world, thereby embracing knowledge that leads to a relationship with the Bible. Without

this fundamental change, the intended devotional character remains beyond reach, and the spiritual life stagnates.

3. "Eternal life," often perceived as a distant promise, is a present reality for those who embrace the Bible's wisdom.[5] This wisdom, also called "Jesus Christ,"[6] liberates from religious error through a costly but rewarding journey of surrender and sacrifice. Through intimate knowledge of *Christ*, the devotional conversation is transformed, empowering it to claim healing promises intended to strengthen the devotional experience.

4. True faith, a gift bestowed upon the ready and willing mind, demands more than intellectual assent. It requires heartfelt commitment to the philosophy of the Bible's intended manner of wellbeing. The path to wellbeing involves a radical departure from the religious world's desires. Embracing *Christ*, which is the devotional conversation's high priest, personal and devotional transformation, although not an easy concept to experience, becomes available.

5. Union with *Christ* signifies a life hidden within the Bible's character, where the conversation is no longer living for its self but for its will, abiding in its love through obedience and exercise. Love is herein demonstrated through faithful adherence to *Christ*, which is but the Bible's present philosophy of personal devotional wellbeing, exemplifying transformation in every aspect of life.

6. The incarnation of the Bible's philosophy within the *flesh*, or within the body of belief, represents the fulfillment of the living God's righteousness within the devotional conversation. The crucifixion of the living God's chief apostle represents the conversation's liberty from the

---

5   Proverbs 3:1,2
6   1 Corinthians 1:24

religious world's spiritual philosophy, attaining sobriety and intelligence through the Bible's wisdom. This transformation demands a separation from influences encouraging religious error, and a dedication to the service of that philosophy of devotional resurrection.

7. The Bible's promises are living truths that cleanse the innermost being, as it is intended that the inward person of the devotional conversation hold the wisdom of the Bible's truth.[7] This wisdom contains material allowing the individual conversation to construct an inward temple. It is within this temple that the living God's devotional character is to live and dwell.

8. The faithful conversation must abstain from anything religiously and spiritually harmful to the mind of its character. This abstinence leads one to embody the Bible's philosophy of newness, becoming a living testimony of it kindness. Written not with ink, but with the Bible's *Mind*,[8] conversations must cultivate a self-sacrificing spirit, adding faith and wisdom to their affection. Without this effort, there will be no personal victories over the natural devotional conscience to advance practical devotional *godliness*.

9. The conscience of the devotional conversation is to become one's the *holy* temple. Allowing the devotional conversation to be renewed in the spirit of its mind,[9] the conversation begins to adopt, as it pertains to the Bible, "holiness." This conversation attains this "holiness" when proving the Bible's intention.[10]

10. An abstemious diet from hurtful religious indulgences, both self-imposed and endorsed by the religious

---

7   Psalm 51:6
8   2 Corinthans 3:3
9   Ephesians 4:23
10   Romans 12:2

world, is the first step toward truly learning how to honor the Bible's devotional character. The will must be stirred to prove the Bible's will through personal chastening, suffering for the sake of mental health and philosophical advancement. True faith is reflected in our belief's determined effort to grow.

11. Before sanctification, there is temperance, humility, and patience. This sequence leads to the conversation's refreshing without self-willed work. The Bible's wisdom within our body of belief results from humbling ourselves to strict self-watch, acknowledging that our sufficiency is the Bible's wisdom .

12. The new mind of devotion, which is generated from being created within the Bible's benevolent understanding,[11] is not just for our devotional conscience, but also for our natural conscience. The illustration given in the eighth chapter of the book of Romans educates the individual conversation on the intended resurrection, how it is to not only benefit the devotional being, but also the human being.[12] The conversation's journey to resurrection through grace is for the stability of our organism.

13. Without advancing in the science of the Bible's will, we remain injured both devotionally and naturally in mind and conscience. Self-sacrifice for inward wellbeing is essential for bearing the fruit of a sound conscience. Ruling one's spirit leads to greater health and prosperity, which "rule" or regulation the Bible's wisdom strengthens.

14. Personal heresies arise when the Bible doesn't feed out devotional conversation. Our conversation's failure to apply the Bible's words leads to a presumptuous stance against faith's higher learning. To refrain from the natural attitude

11   Ephesians 4:24
12   Romans 8:11

within the religious world, which attitude is one neglecting actual insight from the Bible, the devotional conversation needs to update the character of its understanding. As a *building* and *temple*, conversations must consume the words of the Bible, ensuring those words, according to the spirit of the mind,[13] are exercised.

---

13   1 Peter 4:6

3

The Result of An Abstemious Diet

1. As our conversation exists within a religious world that does not serve its best interest, we are called to turn away from religious desires that battle against our personal wellbeing; such a restraint reflects the inward impact of the Bible's philosophy (1 Peter 2:11, 2:15-16). With clear minds, disciplined and sober, we must shed the old spiritual cravings of our past religious ignorance, choosing instead to suffer for what is according to the Bible's character, entrusting our conversation to its Creator (1 Peter 1:13-14, 3:17, 4:19). This path of self-denial is not mere restriction but a testimony of service to understanding, aligning our personal and devotional life with the Bible's eternal purpose.

2. Abstaining from *fleshly* impulses (what spiritually tempts our body of belief) marks us as servants of the Bible's character, quieting both inner and outer ignorance (1 Peter 2:15). The Ten Commandments were given to reveal the conversation's need for higher understanding, stopping every mouth before "truth" (Romans 3:19). Likewise, those conversations embodying these commandments in

their character reflect this same humbling power, shaping a conscience that mirrors structured order (1 Timothy 4:12). By living as examples to other minds, the Bible's counsel works powerfully in us, urging us to guard our hearts diligently, for in doing so, we enlighten ourselves and those who witness our faith (1 Thessalonians 2:13, 1 Timothy 4:16).

3. Enduring hardship for the sake of conscience, as the Bible wills, transforms suffering into a pathway of renewal, turning the heart toward its regenerative purpose over selfish desires (1 Peter 2:19). Overcoming the weaknesses of our natural devotional conversation through faith in the Bible's spiritual understanding proves our allegiance to its *throne*, for a life enslaved to base religious appetite shows a lack of its benefit within (James 3:2). A disciplined life, guided by reason and grace, reveals the power of the Bible's mediation, controlling the tongue of our belief, along with its cravings (James 1:26). Through suffering our body of belief to exist without what falsely stimulates it and our human being, we cease from the Bible's definition of sin, finding blessed hope in the dominion of words over our efforts to live right (1 Peter 4:1, 4:11).

4. The allegory of the suffering linked to the living God's chief apostle sets the pattern for our own transformation (1 Peter 3:18, Romans 6:9-10). The metaphor behind his death and resurrection invites us to die to self and live through the quickening power of the Bible's words (1 Peter 3:18). By embracing this exercising of faith, we confront temptation, beating down injustice with justice, building a foundation in the Bible's will through experimental trust in the mediation of its words for health (1 Peter 4:1). This daily dying to self, paired with reliance on the *Spirit* backing that will, renews the heart, granting life as we commit our person to that will's

keeping, trusting in the power of the living God to resurrect our personal and devotional self (1 Peter 1:21, 4:19).

5. This hope of renewal, first modeled by the living God's chief apostle, anchors our reformation, for as he was in figure raised to die no more, our conversation can also rise above religious error in heart and in deed, experiencing the power of the Bible's words to transform us (Romans 6:9, 1 Peter 1:21). Through sanctification by understanding, our belief is reborn as it executes learned wisdom (1 Peter 1:2, 1:22-23). By embracing the doctrine revealed to our conversation, it is begotten anew, our belief shaped by wisdom to reflect the nature of the Bible's intention for our inward person (Ephesians 1:4, 1 John 3:24).

6. Temperance is the gateway to this transformation, for by monitoring the operation of our body of belief, we fulfill the Bible's will of having our conversation healthy and informed (1 Thessalonians 4:3, 1 Peter 3:11). This type of suffering put onto our conversation enabling us to rightly know what we would either live or die for (1 Peter 4:1). This discipline builds confidence in the Bible, cultivating the kindness of a refreshed personal and devotional character (Titus 3:4). Only through such self-denial can we hear its voice clearly, refraining from spiritual negligence to do right by our self (1 Thessalonians 5:23).

7. The message, "Bind up the testimony, seal the law among my disciples," demands a temperate life, for intemperance clouds the mind, blocking the Bible's counsel (Isaiah 8:16). The mortality of our conversation is replaced with an unending experience when we are able to learn of, know, and put an end to harmful devotional habits (2 Corinthians 5:4, Romans 8:13-14). This exercise, perfected in conscience, flows from knowing what the Bible calls the conversation to

suffer for, allowing it to embrace a faith that is simple and personally serviceable (Hebrews 9:9, 1 Peter 1:15, 5:1).

8. True faith unites us with the Bible's intention for our devotional experience (1 Peter 1:3, John 17:23). Without educating and refining our mental, moral, and philosophical diet, we cannot maintain a sure relationship with the Bible's advice (1 Timothy 6:3). By humbly accepting our faith's higher learning, we receive more grace for our belief's creation, advancing toward the intended conversation in every right way (James 4:6, 2 Corinthians 10:5, 1 Peter 1:15).

4

The Meat Of The Body

1. The soul's clarity hinges on the focus of its under-standing, even like as it says, "The light of the body is the eye: if therefore thine eye be single, thy whole body shall be full of light" (Matthew 6:22-23). A mind anchored in the Bible's truth radiates healthy wisdom throughout one's being, but a heart swayed by selfish spiritual desires plunges into darkness, unable to properly serve both that wisdom and self (Matthew 6:24). To obsess, in right context, over earthly religious needs; what to eat, drink, or wear; betrays a lack of trust in the care of our conversation's Creator, for "is not the life more than meat, and the body than raiment?" (Matthew 6:25, 6:31). True devotional maturity surpasses mere sustenance, rooted in a faith that aligns the soul with *heaven's* purpose.

2. A heart given to appetite, chasing self-reliance, feeds on an "evil eye," provoking endless worries: "What shall we eat? or, What shall we drink? or, Wherewithal shall we be clothed?" (Proverbs 23:6, Matthew 6:31). Such gluttony stems from ignorance of the Bible's power, dismissing its

wisdom as "less than nothing" or "a strange thing" (Isaiah 40:17, Hosea 8:12). Yet, those who embrace God's voice as "good to the use of edifying" find health through chastening, their souls turning from useless religious pleasures to the meaning of a fulfilled devotional experience (Ephesians 4:29, Job 33:19-20, 33:29-30). By choosing the nourishment from the Bible over religious cravings from outside of the Bible, the heart is drawn from the pit of its self, enlightened by the fact kept hidden at the Bible's core.

3. The *eye* of understanding determines our spiritual diet; whether we consume meaningless desires of the flesh (of the body of our belief) or the enduring wisdom of the Bible through faith in its *name* (Ephesians 1:18). Remaining mindful of earthly religious needs reveals a lack of trust in the living Bible's living *Mind*, unlike the lilies of the field, which bloom without toil, guided by a natural will through seasons of growth and renewal (Matthew 6:28, 6:30). Spiritual intemperance is contrary to the new covenant's will, which will tasks the devotional conversation with exercising faith on the Bible's words (1 Timothy 4:7-8). Faithless rituals based in religious law and tradition lead to the corruption of our belief, while a single focus on the Bible's *Spirit* reaps an unending connection to it source of life for our devotional conscience (Galatians 6:8).

4. Through this *Spirit's* grace, we gain "power everlasting," a strength born through interacting with the Bible's wisdom (1 Timothy 6:16, Ecclesiastes 7:19). Only by embracing this wisdom can we cease fretting over earthly spiritual needs, allowing the law of the mediation of this wisdom within our heart and mind to transform our faith's conscience (1 Timothy 4:8). The same creative power, which holds all things together, will reshape our lives; the key is to allow that creative power to work through its credible outlet

(Colossians 1:17). Experimenting with the Bible's words frees us from "philosophy and vain deceit," filling our hearts with rivers of living water (John 8:36, Colossians 2:8, John 7:38-39).

5. Yet, if our understanding is clouded by religious desires, "how great is that darkness!" (Matthew 6:23). A diet rooted in self leads to spiritual ruin, even like as it says, "Thy sorrow is incurable for the multitude of thine iniquity" (Jeremiah 30:15). The Bible knows which conversations mock its intellect and which conversations intended to heal form it. (Galatians 6:7, 2 Timothy 2:19, John 6:64). A sensual mind spirals into numb spiritual decay, its wound deemed incurable (Micah 1:9). Conversations professing the Bible's *name* yet clinging to spiritual intemperance cannot grasp the truth at its core (John 15:5, 2 Timothy 3:7). Their god becomes their belly, their glory their shame, as they chase what the religious world offers for answers (Philippians 3:19, Romans 16:18).

6. Bearing the Bible's *name* requires removing the devotional self away from what it defines as "sin" (2 Timothy 2:19, Romans 6:5, 6:11). World religious bondage belongs to conversations that will not accept a sober relationship with the Bible's words. (2 Timothy 3:2-4, Galatians 4:3, Titus 1:1). A heart full of religious desires leaves no room for the healing light of wisdom's revelation, rendering faith vain by taking the Bible's understanding in futility (Titus 1:16, 2 Timothy 3:5). We are counseled to turn from such an unprofitable experience, avoiding "winebibbers" and "riotous eaters of flesh" (or those that would enflame themselves on the *knowledge* springing from the own religious understanding that is based in religious tradition); spiritual intemperance fuels a dead religion, born of faithless anxiety (Proverbs 23:20, Matthew 6:31).

7. The path to a restful and fulfilling devotional conversation lies in our learning solely from an experimental experience with the Bible. Like a seed that dies to bear fruit, we must let go of our devotional self to possess a quickened conversation, which is why it says, "He that hateth his life in this world shall keep it unto life eternal" (John 12:24, 12:25, 1 Corinthians 15:36). This "eternal life" comes through dying to the mindless desires of the body of our belief and embracing the wisdom at the center of the Bible (John 17:3, 1 Timothy 6:16). By sacrificing the *eye* of indulgence through love and faith, we gain the knowledge of sanctification, joining our obedience to the creative power of grace until we reach the intended devotional character (Ephesians 4:13).

5

The Life Diet

1. The food we choose shapes more than our bodies; it shapes our spiritual character, determining whether we live for what fades or for what endures. The message of the living God's chief apostle us is one calling its hearer to labor not for perishable *meat*, but for the bread that brings unending edification (John 6:27, 51). This is no ordinary sustenance; it's the living bread from "heaven," or from an experience with the core of the scripture's Mind, promising a devotional renewal that a *death* by religion cannot touch (John 6:50). To therefore eat this man's flesh and drink his blood is to take in the very essence emboldening his conversation's conscience (John 6:55). Yet, clinging to the natural devotional conversation's diet; those inherited spiritual cravings and religious traditions; leads only to the decay of our belief, even like as it is warned: "If you live after the flesh (after the motivations of the body of the belief), you shall die" (Romans 8:13, 1 Peter 1:18).

2. The heart, swayed by its own desires, will chases mindless theological pleasures, wandering into spiritual leanness and

confusion (Psalm 81:12, 106:15). It follows its own counsel, blind to the Bible's reality, lured by what is ultimately false (Numbers 15:39). The wise conversations, however, keep their *eyes* fixed on the path of the Bible's intention, while those who reject it slide backward, lost in their own imaginations (Ecclesiastes 2:14, Psalm 81:11, Jeremiah 7:24). To choose the *life diet* is to reject this vain inheritance, to turn from the heart's deceit and seek nourishment that endures.

3. The living God's chief apostle, through his willing sacrifice, philosophically broke the chains of human ordinances (Ephesians 2:15, Colossians 2:14). The allegory behind his crucifixion reveals an abolishment of religion's old way; decrees handed down and believed on by priests and mediators; not just for this time, but also for all time (Ephesians 1:21, Galatians 3:19). His spilled blood evinces the plague of religious legalism binding the devotional conscience, offering instead a new diet led by the message of his ministry, which diet brings newness of mind to those who hear and experiment with it (John 5:24). Through actively exercising faith in this wisdom, we receive power to regenerate the body of our belief (John 1:12). This power reshapes our faith's conscience, allowing our conversation to embrace the redemption purposed, even like as it says, "Christ hath redeemed us from the curse of the law" (Galatians 3:13).

4. The eternal life of our belief's consciousness is the Bible's gift to us, a peace that flows from grace through faith (Romans 6:23, 5:1, Ephesians 2:8). To eat this bread of understanding is to let the allegory of his death and resurrection both flood and transform our heart (John 4:14). Without it, we lack the wisdom of the Bible's will to perceive the type of *death* it asks us to comply with (Philippians 3:10). Feeding on the *flesh's* (the religious conversation's) traditions; those inherited and self-cultivated theories and superstitions; binds

us to a form of mental spiritual slavery (the Bible's ultimate definition of "death"), leaving our faith bitter and empty (Romans 5:12, Acts 8:23). But the message at the core of the scriptures, because it adds life to our body of belief, delivers us from religious darkness, translating us into the *kingdom* of counsel, where wisdom and understanding reign (Colossians 1:13, 1:9). This experience strengthens our faith and gives us every reason to follow and trust the Bible's wisdom (Hebrews 4:16, 1 Corinthians 1:30).

5. The Bible's will is our belief's sanctification, a call to abstain from the fornication of false worship and to choose the *meat* of its fact (1 Thessalonians 4:3). This "meat"; the knowledge of its will for our conversation; brings nourishment not only to us, but also to others, as we grow fond of it (2 Thessalonians 2:13). To eat it is to grow in temperance, to love the jealous care that the Bible's living Mind has for our inward person (Proverbs 2:10-11). Unlike Saul, who chased his own desires, we're called to David's path, bound to the living God's life through wisdom and love (1 Samuel 23:20, 25:29). What we learn from interacting with the Bible will strengthens us, ensuring our belief's moral and spiritual recovery through disciplined faith (John 6:57, Ephesians 3:20).

6. The sacrifice of the living God's chief apostle shows the cost of religious error; his body of understanding crucified, metaphorically accursed for us, bearing the weight of a human-ordained spiritual experience (Deuteronomy 21:23, 1 Corinthians 15:56). His death ended the power stimulating a false religion, offering a new diet: the philosophy embedded within his message's disposition, the only sustenance for those *dead* to the religious world's culture (Luke 23:46, Colossians 2:20). To love the Bible's *Spirit* is to live by its counsels, to let its character shape and re-shape every

step (2 John 1:6). Feeding on the desires of our natural body of belief leaves us in the *death* of misunderstanding, but the diet of the Bible's words brings *life*, freeing us from the curse of spiritual negligence (Romans 5:12).

7. The reformer's hope lies in this diet, holding fast to the mediation of the meaning within the example set by the living God's chief apostle (Hebrews 3:6). Our joy is a clear devotional conscience, rooted in sincerity and fervent service to the Bible's intended devotional experience (2 Corinthians 1:12, Romans 12:11). Grace builds a character that's sober, just, and renewed, quiet in the peace of the Bible's instruction (Titus 1:8, Romans 14:17). This work isn't passive; it's a work of love and a labor of hope powered by a confidence in the Bible's character (1 Thessalonians 1:3, 1:5). Rejecting this experience will lead to one calling the Bible false, to render its philosophy void (1 John 5:10, Romans 3:3). Conversations rooted in a personal experience with the Bible let go of old religious desires and become renewed in will and in understanding, alive to the Bible's wisdom (Galatians 5:24, Romans 6:11).

8. The allegory of his resurrection proves the defeat of death (of the philosophy of the religious law) to be true and ultimately necessary (Romans 6:9, 1 Corinthians 15:56). We're called to reckon ourselves dead to religious error, free from spiritual bondage, alive through the example of his act (Romans 8:15, 8:13). This diet of his example's philosophy transforms us, renewing our minds to reflect the image of its brilliance, sustained by a devotional life that never fades (Ephesians 4:23, Colossians 3:10). This is the meaning of eternal life. To choose it is to embrace a path of discipline, to let the Bible's reality nourish our belief into an experience of *godliness*, whole and unending.

6

The Appointed Work
of Reformation

1. The human heart, rough and unyielding by nature, finds its transformation not in its own strength, but through the philosophy put into the allegory of the living God's chief apostle. For the conversation trusting unwaveringly in the *name* of this philosophy, a meaningful truth emerges: "I am crucified with Christ: nevertheless I live; yet not I, but Christ liveth in me" (Galatians 2:20). This is the cornerstone of temperance; a life surrendered, where the old devotional self dies, and the understanding of the living God's chief apostle lives within, guiding the reformer to live by that wisdom, rooted in its love and kindness. True reformation begins here, with the conscious choice to die to self and let this counsel take root, shaping every thought and action through faith in its redemptive power.

2. Temperance is no shallow restraint; it's a deep, deliberate act of aligning the devotional conscience with the Bible's message. The heart must first feel its own sickness; its bent

toward religious error; before it can seek true healing (Galatians 2:20). Without this manner of conviction, driven by loose imagination rather than sturdy reason, any attempt at reform falters. The flesh (the body of our belief), unchecked, rules both within and without, trapping the inward person in a cycle of self-deception that masquerades as comfort (Ephesians 4:22). But when the heart acknowledges its need, it opens to a reformation guided by the wisdom of the Bible's character, not the whims stimulated by our natural religious conscience.

3. The call to reformation is clear, to keep both the Bible's core message and counsels (Revelation 14:12). This is the path to an experience in the "kingdom and patience" of the living God's chief apostle (Revelation 1:9). Faith alone isn't enough; it must be paired with virtue, knowledge, and patience, each building on the other to shape a devotional life of discretion (Ephesians 4:23). Without the testimony of the Bible's will etched in the heart of our understanding, there will be no drive to re-educate the body of our understanding, no hunger for a better way (Romans 6:6). The Bible urges us to shed the old religious self, to renew the devotional mind, and to embrace a life governed by learned truth (Ephesians 4:22-23).

4. To declare, "I am crucified with Christ," is to embrace the allegory of his death and resurrection, to own a conversation now planted in the likeness of his conversation and raised to new life (Romans 6:5). He died to define justification, and to expose the spirit backing conversations guided by religious law, so that we might exist free from its grip (Romans 4:25, 6:6). Sin, rooted in legalism and human religious tradition, has no hold where faith in the philosophy of death and resurrections reigns (Romans 6:9, 14:23). This manner of belief demands an active choice to live by the

revelation given through his suffering, to let his sacrifice re-define our conversation, free from the religious world's empty guidelines (Galatians 3:12).

5. Wisely and benevolently keeping the Bible's commandments was at the heart of that man's message, a love expressed through an intelligent obedience (1 John 5:3). But without embracing the philosophy tied to living God's chief apostle, our efforts remain motivated by our physical body's stimulus, lacking reason or purpose (Romans 8:2, 2 Corinthians 4:4). The mediation of that philosophy offers devotional freedom to personally know the Bible, but only if we surrender to it, letting its grace re-order our hearts (Hebrews 5:13). Without this, our profession of faith becomes presumption, a hollow claim with no power to transform.

6. Grace is the tide that lifts the heart, stirring it to yield to will of the Bible's *Mind* (Ephesians 1:9). When we grasp the depth of its love, the heart softens, ready to follow its purpose (John 7:17). This love, displayed in the living God's chief apostle's death, reveals the Bible's character, inviting us to know and honor it (Romans 8:2). Devotional perfection does not come from human effort but from experimenting with the power of the Bible's words, letting its *Spirit* guide every step (Galatians 2:20). The reformer's reality is this: to learn of and do the will of its counsel, free from the chains of spiritual sin and death (free from the chains of religious law).

7. It is our right to examine the body of our belief, to know if it matches up to the belief at the Bible's core. (2 Corinthians 13:5). Where sin abounds, grace overflows, enabling us to be temperate in our personal and devotional desires (Romans 5:20, 1 Corinthians 9:25). To live by the Bible's *Faith* is to let its life shine through our conversation, a testimony of the benefit of having our understanding crucified and renewed

(Galatians 2:20). Without this framework, the heart clings to unjust spiritual impulses, mistaking faith's *death* for spiritual wellness (1 Corinthians 15:56). The soul untouched by the Bible's truth remains lost to its own sensibilities, unable to break free from inherited and self-conceived personal and devotional lies (Proverbs 2:11).

8. Religious error (sin) reigns where the impulses of the spiritual body rules (Romans 6:12, 6:19). The *body*, alive to its desires, leads only to ruin (Romans 8:10, 6:21). But through the Bible's counsel we put these deeds to sleep, finding life in understanding how to approach our belief (Romans 8:13). Learning through the living God's chief apostle means conquering the body of our faith with instruction, letting that knowledge govern every act (Galatians 2:20). The humility given by this wisdom sets the pattern, preserving us through discretion and understanding (Philippians 2:8, Proverbs 2:11).

9. This grace, a gift of devotional life and refreshing, calls us to sacrifice, to join those who covenant with the Mind of the scriptures through surrender (1 Peter 3:7, Psalm 50:5). By this wisdom, we overcome the impulses of an undisciplined spiritual body, letting its voice triumph through faith (Romans 6:12). As this wisdom was in the living God's chief apostle, so it will also work in us, bettering our devotional understanding through its imprint (2 Corinthians 5:19, 5:21). This is the reformer's task: to live by the faith of the Bible's counsel, to let its *Spirit* shape a life of love and liberty, being confident that "God is with us" (Isaiah 8:10). In this, the heart finds its true *home*, renewed and whole, sustained by the power of an unending grace.

7

Godly Living Through
The Power Of Wisdom

1. The pursuit of "godly living" begins with reverence towards the words within the Bible, as it says, "The fear of the LORD is the beginning of wisdom" (Proverbs 9:10). Wisdom directs the conversation's thoughts and feelings and brings our experience to light, leading us in unique paths of character development (Ecclesiastes 10:10, Proverbs 8:20). Without embracing the wisdom given from the Bible, without hiding its counsels in our hearts and applying our minds to its fact, our faith falters in growing in a grace that leads to the knowledge of the Bible's saving intention (2 Peter 3:18, Proverbs 2:1-2).

2. The living God's truth is the law of his philosophy on our faith's resurrection, which is why it says, "Thy law is the truth," and, "The law is light" (Psalm 119:142, Proverbs 6:23). A wise heart hears and obeys what it learns from the Bible, increasing in learning as it aligns with the "law of the Spirit of life" (Romans 8:2, Proverbs 1:5). Such obedience

yields a demeanor correctly representing the experience, which is why it says, "The words of a wise man's mouth are gracious" (Ecclesiastes 10:12). By learning and living every word from the Bible's *Spirit*, the soul attains wise counsel, preserving itself through what it retains (Proverbs 1:5, 2:11, 3:21). Wisdom strengthens the heart, taming its contrary impulses, and keeps the conversation under vigilant watch, encouraging a mindful spirit within the soul's temple.

3. The purpose of growing in grace and in knowledge is singular: The Bible's wisdom is our personal and devotional support (Proverbs 4:22). Wisdom is, to the Bible's mind, life itself, which is why it says that "she is thy life" and "shall preserve thee" when loved and cherished (Proverbs 4:6, 4:13). Through obedience to its instruction, we grasp its strength, finding peace, for it declares, "Take hold of my strength, that he may make peace with me" (Isaiah 27:5). In our weakness, its grace suffices, perfecting strength to sustain our conversation (2 Corinthians 12:9). Only by yielding to the Bible's mindful influence do its thoughts for us bear fruit, as "when wisdom entereth into thine heart, and knowledge is pleasant unto thy soul; discretion shall preserve thee, understanding shall keep thee" (Proverbs 2:10,11).

4. This wisdom begins with humility, for "God resisteth the proud, and giveth grace to the humble," blessing the intention of the conversation desiring to be well (1 Peter 5:5, Proverbs 3:33-34). Reverence for the Bible's living Mind, the root of wisdom, imparts understanding as the conversation refrains from what it defines as "evil" (Proverbs 9:10, Job 28:28). By applying the Bible's words practically, the believer ends the reign of "evil" within their conversation, ceasing unprofitable spiritual indulgences through the Bible's guidance (Proverbs 9:9). While self-reliant efforts risk failure, those governed by wisdom proclaim, "I can do all things

through Christ which strengtheneth me" (1 Corinthians 10:12, Philippians 4:13). The Bible's words, when lived, produce fruit, increasing knowledge and fortifying the soul against the natural tendencies of an unrefined devotional conversation.

5. Overcoming the crude impulses of the devotional body requires diligent application of the Bible's philosophical context, for "it shall be health to thy navel, and marrow to thy bones" when we humble ourselves to seek its counsel (Proverbs 3:8). Conversations that hate its instruction, loving *death* (numbness of the spiritual mind), reject life (an unending dialogue with the Bible's understanding) (Proverbs 8:36). Wisdom and discretion flush out spiritual corruption, replacing self-sufficiency with active strength (Proverbs 8:33). The "godly soul," desiring to reflect the Bible's character, embraces correction (Revelation 3:19, Proverbs 3:11). Through willing obedience to what one learns from the scriptures, the heart is renewed, cleansed from double-mindedness, earning its "crown of life" (James 4:8, Jude 1:24, James 1:12).

6. Love for the Bible's living Mind is shown through keeping the commandments reflecting that Mind's character; "if ye love me, keep my commandments," it says (John 14:15, 14:24). Health is promised to faithful conversations, crowning them with the substance of grace for creation (Exodus 20:6, Proverbs 4:9). By subjecting the body of our belief to the Bible's precepts, we become partakers of its glory, perfected through patient inward *suffering* (1 Peter 4:19, James 1:4). Wisdom multiplies the days of our faith's intellect, granting "grace and peace" through knowledge (Proverbs 9:11, 2 Peter 1:2). Diligent obedience to what we personally learn from the Bible procures this favor (Proverbs 11:27, 9:10).

7. Yet, many conversations reject this experience, for "Israel hath cast off the thing that is good," forgetting their faith's Maker by ignoring the wisdom found within words (Hosea 8:3, 8:14). Emboldening a belief founded upon flesh-based or sensual offerings, they neglect the Creator's power, refusing to experiment with the Bible's "fear" (Hosea 8:13, Jeremiah 5:22). This lack of reverence stifles spiritual growth, leaving the belief estranged (Proverbs 1:29-30, Psalm 81:11). Ungodliness (a reliance on religious laws and traditions) persists when the heart resists the Bible's influence, but through grace we can put off the "body of the sins of the flesh" (or we can put off a devotional conversation unjustly governed) (Romans 3:24, Colossians 2:11). It is through rightly examining the scriptures that our conversation regains the rest that it has surrendered to the religious world (2 Timothy 2:15, Hebrews 3:18).

8. This rest, found in meditating on the Bible's conscience, edifies the conversation's inward person, enabling it to walk "in the fear of the Lord, and in the comfort of the Holy Ghost" (Acts 9:31). Abiding in the safety of this revelation, we confess, "We have known and believed the love that God hath to us"; "God is love" (1 John 4:16, 2 Corinthians 13:14). This love purges the conscience of our conversation from dead religious works, granting "abundance of grace and of the gift of righteousness" through its wisdom (Hebrews 9:14, Romans 5:17). If we want a "righteous" conversation, wisdom leads the way, saying, "I lead in the way of righteousness"; without it, the Bible's intention cannot flourish (Proverbs 8:20, 9:10).

9. The conversation, diseased by an issue from its conception within the religious world, finds healing in its relationship with the Bible (Matthew 9:20, Leviticus 15:2, Colossians 1:21-22, Romans 8:11). To follow it's frame of thought, we

must consistently deny our natural religious self, taking up its *cross* to retain its words, even like as it says, "Let thine heart retain my words: keep my commandments, and live" (Luke 9:23, Proverbs 4:4). Without reform, no devotional revival can take root; without humbling the heart to the precepts of the Bible's philosophy, its *light* remains dim, for "the commandment is a lamp" (Proverbs 6:23). By embracing self-denial, eating purely from the Bible's hand, we magnify its words, knowing our belief's Maker through a living faith that transforms the conversation into a vessel of its glory.

8

Living By His Mercies

1. In the context of Paul's exhortation,[14] the Bible's students are urged to present their *bodies*, or their devotional conversations, as fit and living sacrifices to the living God. This call to sacrificial living is considered the student's reasonable service, highlighting that sincere devotional worship involves our belief possessing a health conscience. The sacrifices we offer must be living, not dead, and rooted in a consciousness aligned with *creation's* grace. When we neglect to apply this consciousness to our life, we disregard the purpose of our faith's creation, leading to spiritual waywardness and deviation from right inward devotion.

2. Paul emphasizes the necessity of self-correction and adherence to a faith that is gained through experience, urging his audience to conduct themselves in a manner befitting the science of the Bible's philosophy. The sacrifices pleasing to that philosophy involve a broken or penitent

14   Romans 12:1

spirit and a renewed mind.[15] Without this renewal, we cannot offer the necessary sacrifices for a right experience with the scriptures. The command to work out our own salvation by the renewing of our minds underscores the importance of patiently growing with the Bible, giving to it the *body* of our belief as living a proof of spiritual vitality.

3. The process of devotional rebirth and renewal echoes the living God's power, whose *voice* intelligently conducted all things into existence. This same power intends to consume our belief its patience and longsuffering for growth and development, transforming it's understanding, through its suffering, into the image of its devotional character. The life of our spirit, or the energy of our faith's mind, thrives even in the bitterness of our soul; it is only as we embrace the power of grace do we grow in practical spiritual godliness. By believing in and adhering to the wisdom we retain when examining the Bible's character, we maintain a conversation that reflects correct devotional principles.

4. The conversation of the Bible's student is counseled to be holy and without blemish, aspiring to a learning experience without spot or wrinkle, or without deviating and entertaining what is philosophically negligent. This requires dependence on the wisdom and power of the Bible's individual ministry. Paul teaches that godliness and *bodily* reformation come by the living God's mercies. Without acknowledging these mercies, we cannot offer transformative *sacrifices* that create our conversation anew. The *flesh*, or the body of our belief, engaged with death and bound by legal religious traditions, cannot please the mind at the core of the scriptures. True service to that *Mind* involves seeking what is above and beyond the religious world, even turning

15   Psalm 51:10,17

to the living God's right hand, where the conversation of the living God's chief apostle sits.

5. The psalmist calls for praise from the *waters* above the *heavens*.[16] The psalmist is, figuratively, referring to an assembly, as "waters" are a figurative illustration for an assembly, congregation, or host.[17] Spiritual conversations must overcome *fleshly* indulgences, or the deadening of philosophical and devotional perception by embracing "mercies", which "mercies" are a promised covenant of peace,[18] showers of blessing outpouring to the mind that will set its thoughts and feelings in order. These showers of blessings come to those who form a covenant with the living God through sacrifice,[19] enabling the living God's mercies to defeat every reckless religious indulgence.

6. Spiritual sacrifices, if they should be accepted, require a sacrifice through covenant, making the body of our belief an acceptable present to the living God's *name*. Through the mediation of the Bible's philosophy, we receive spiritual blessings to offer acceptable sacrifices, honoring the intended devotional experience while refreshing our faith's intellect and overcoming sensual religious inclinations. A stubborn refusal to meet *creation's* requirements indicates a rival god within that strives for mastery over our being.

7. False professions of faith, without an intelligent expression of devotional wellbeing, lead to spiritual devastation. Conversations failing to strengthen the body of their belief will receive strong religious error and delusion. "Sin," which is defined as "unrighteousness,"[20] is strengthened by the

---

16   Psalm 148:4
17   Revelation 17:5; Isaiah 60:5
18   Isaiah 55:3
19   Psalm 50:5
20   1 John 5:17

philosophy of the religious law.[21] An unintelligent expression of faith is an expression that is dictated through religious laws, which expression the death of the living God's chief apostle brings to light. True godliness, and with a willing mind desiring counsel, involves the devotional conversation humbly experiencing the will at the center of the scriptures.

8. Intemperance ruins a sincere profession of faith in *creation's* science. Solomon's regret over his *indulgences* serves as a warning. To have *bodies* that are presentable, conversations must maintain soundness through self-sacrifice and self-discipline. Grace, which is the balm of all creation, combined with personal willpower, enables overcoming inherited and self-cultivated personal and devotional defects through patience and longsuffering.

9. The conversation's spirit or conscience, like as a candle is to darkness, is ordained to search the inward parts.[22] A proven and tested will fosters integrity and strength. Perfect peace is promised to the conversation whose mind is steadfast on the intended journey, drawing strength from the living God's *words*. Without the *peace* and *mercies* of these words, the essence of our conversation's character will deplete, leading to regretful religious indulgences and spiritual lethargy. Justification, which is the process of our conversation's regeneration, enables our belief to inherit the intended *eternal life*, replacing its mortal frame with an immortal *body*.

10. Experiencing the power of the Bible's words and maintaining a conversation aligned with its wisdom requires a conscious decision to adopt its mind. The pattern of Adam, who slept to allow the *Word* to work within *him*, exemplifies the conversation's surrender to wisdom. Abounding in hope through the living God's *Mind*, conversations must be filled

---

21   1 Corinthians 15:56
22   Proverbs 20:27

with goodness, knowledge, and spiritual understanding, presenting themselves as living sacrifices, quickened by its science.

11. Self-restraint and a commitment to the spiritual values at core of the scriptures are essential for advancing in devotional "godliness." Renewal in knowledge means continual self-correction and active trust in in those values. Present transformation, rather than future reformation, is necessary for pure and undefiled communication with the intended experience. Thoughts regulate actions, and a mind committed to *creation's* will leads to godly living.

12. Conversations are to abstain from devotional fornication, idolatry, and adultery, rejecting the naturally indulgent and sensual nature of their *bodies*. True godliness involves, to the detriment of our natural religious *frame*, obedience to the precepts we learn from the Bible.[23] Our reasonable service involves bearing the sufferings of the living God's chief apostle, who gave the spirit of his belief's mind, that he may join the ranks of them that uphold *creation's* will, to the promise of consolation for personal and devotional wellbeing.

13. The blessings of the new covenant bring personal contact with the living God, and refusing the intended covenant experience means failing to possess the philosophy of godliness. To serve the living God, conversations must refrain from *fleshly* ordinances and embrace the scripture's present will, leading to a life of devotional love, liberty, and reconciliation. The Bible's counsel calls for abstinence from religious error, encouraging a kind and healthy devotional lifestyle through the grace and mercies of the living God.

---

23   1 Corinthians 2:14

9

Surrendering To One Diet

1. Life flows through the blood, pulsing in every part of us, but the kind of life we nurture within our devotional body depends on what we feed our hearts (Leviticus 17:11,14). A sound heart brings vitality, while a heart fed on religious corruption breeds *death* (Proverbs 14:30). Scripture urges us to turn from idols, from "blood," from what's "strangled," and from "fornication"; choices that guard our devotional experience and keeps our faith's conscience (Acts 15:20,29). To sow to the flesh, or to the body of our belief, is to reap spiritual decay, but to sow things inwardly illuminating the scriptures yields *life* that lasts forever (Galatians 6:8). The call is clear: plant righteousness and harvest mercy, because spiritual negligence only reaps ruin (Hosea 10:12,13).

2. Two paths lie before us: one feeds the heart with truth, the other with the fleeting religious or spiritual desires. Each choice shapes our faith's conscience, either blessing or cursing those around us (2 Corinthians 2:16, Psalm 73:26). The heart of our belief drives the "flesh" (or body) of our belief, and if we let its unchecked cravings rule, we cry out in

distress, lost in our own longing (Psalm 84:2). A sound heart, though, steadies us, choosing *life* over *death* by guarding what we take in (Proverbs 14:30). To live godly is to regulate these desires, to choose a diet that strengthens the conversation's soul rather than starves it.

3. The Bible's student faces two diets: one leads to death, the other to eternal *life* (2 Corinthians 2:16). Feeding on the offerings of our belief's *body* (idols, blood or unlawful stimulus driving belief, human doctrines) breeds impurity, clouding the mind with restlessness (Acts 15:29, Colossians 2:22). Covetousness, the root of idolatry, stirs a craving that drowns out the Bible's voice, as it did before the flood when their hearts chased only evil (Colossians 3:5, Romans 7:7, Genesis 6:5). Such a diet poisons the spirit of the mind, birthing violence and corruption, as seen in Noah's day when that priesthood carried cruelty, and the *earth* groaned under their rebellion (Genesis 6:11, Psalm 27:12, Jeremiah 6:7).

4. Those lost to this path denied the living God, their hearts corrupt, their lives a flood of negligence (Psalm 14:1, Genesis 6:5). They fed on violence, choosing self over the philosophy at the core of the scriptures. To cling to these idols is to reject the philosophical implications guiding the Bible's core, to cherish what's false over what's true. The heart's natural bent whispers we can be gods, but this lie only binds us to the death of our understanding (Genesis 3:5, Isaiah 57:10). True reform begins with turning away, choosing a diet of soundness over the blood of rebellion.

5. Before we can know the meaning behind the living God's chief apostle's ministry, we must face our own poverty, leaning on the grace of creation to see our devotional flaws clearly (Romans 7:22). Without this, the body of our belief consumes its own desires, building hollow systems to prop itself up, blind to their futility (Psalm 119:126). The heart

must feel its need, its brokenness, before it can embrace the life Bible's philosophy offers (1 Thessalonians 4:3). Grace restores us, not through our own strength, but through obedience to gained understanding, which quickens the soul and aligns it with creation's will (Acts 15:11, Romans 7:22).

6. Feeding on idols; whether lust, pride, or human religious creeds; keeps us chained to *death* (Acts 15:20). This "blood" of the heart, the life of selfish desire, pulls us back to Eve's deception, away from real sanctifying fact (Genesis 6:5, Genesis 3:5). To eat this is to choose devotional corruption, to let the religion's lies govern us (Deuteronomy 12:23). It's a path of delusion, where we crucify the living God's chief apostle anew, rejecting the meaning of that sacrifice for our own misguided strength (Hebrews 6:6, 2 Thessalonians 2:11).

7. The law of the God's philosophy, written on our hearts, calls us to a different diet, one that shapes us for usefulness (Jeremiah 31:33, Exodus 13:16). To learn from the Bible is to come to its wisdom, to let its truth remake us (John 6:45). This is no mere ritual; it's a transformation, a reformation of heart and mind through the creative power of grace (Ephesians 1:13). The living God's chief apostle once thought for us to be kept in this truth, sanctified by our Father's *name*, alive through faith (John 17:11, 2 Thessalonians 2:13). To resist this is to kill the present work of creation, choosing unnecessary conflict over peace (Ephesians 4:21).

8. The Bible's words are life, quickening the dead devotional conversation, breathing health into its numbness (Ephesians 2:1, John 6:63). To eat the flesh of the living God's chief apostle (his understanding) and drink his blood is to let his philosophy reshape us, replacing the heart's old spiritual cravings with his devotional ambition (John 6:55). This isn't a one-time act but a daily choice, a diet of obedience that

builds faith through experience (Ephesians 4:23). Without it, we consume our own destruction, led by lies that promise life but deliver death (1 Timothy 4:1, 1 Corinthians 15:50).

9. The reformer's heart, born of the conscience at the heart of the Bible, chooses this new diet, letting its truth govern every thought (Galatians 1:16). The living God's chief apostle provides a life-giving wisdom, offering us that *life* over the *death* we inherited through religious tradition (1 Corinthians 15:45). To believe on that wisdom is to suffer for the experience that he died for, to let that character strengthen us, filling us with understanding to live as he once did (Philippians 1:29, Ephesians 3:16-17, Colossians 1:9).

10. This path demands surrender, letting go of the devotional body's diet to embrace a diet of mental and spiritual wellbeing. It's a life of discipline, of choosing the Bible's character over self, knowing that only its wisdom brings true health (Colossians 3:10). The heart that yields to this finds peace, not in lame pleasures, but in a soundness that lasts, shaped by the unending grace given through the effort to simply receive, learn, and apply to the Bible's words.

10

Practical Godliness Made Plain Though Practical Wisdom

1. The Bible will never leave our conversation's inward person malnourished, which is why it says, "The LORD will not suffer the soul of the righteous to famish" (Proverbs 10:3). A spirit that is kind to its self brings health to its devotional character, while cruelty towards self leads to a troubled body of faith; "the merciful man doeth good to his own soul" and "he that is cruel troubleth his own flesh" (Proverbs 11:17). The wise heart, diligently seeking good, procures the favor for doing so, receiving counsels to fortify their experience, learning that "the wise in heart will receive commandments" and "wise men lay up knowledge" (Proverbs 10:8, 10:14). Our faith's labor for understanding will in turn transform us into an agent of consolation for another (Proverbs 10:11, 11:30), yet conversations refusing correction are rendered useless, their error occurring due to them failing to practically apply what they have retained from the Bible (Proverbs 10:17, 10:21).

2. The key to a happy devotional conversation is understanding; "understanding is a wellspring of life unto him that hath it" and "the knowledge of the holy is understanding" (Proverbs 16:22, 9:10, Job 28:28). Without willingly experimenting with the Bible's wisdom, many conversations perish, their lives like "water spilt on the ground, which cannot be gathered up again" (2 Samuel 14:14, Jeremiah 11:8). The godly conversation, however, departs from what the Bible defines as evil, restraining its thoughts and feelings for the peace that comes with a sound and a still mind (Proverbs 10:19, 11:12). Trusting in religious wealth or troubling one's own body of belief leads to ruin, but wisdom encourages health and liberty within the conversation's soul temple (Proverbs 11:28, 11:29).

3. Spiritual death stems from laziness to meditate on and execute the Bible's words, but the wise conversation, embracing correction, bears fruit as a tree of life, for wisdom "is a tree of life to them that lay hold upon her" (Proverbs 3:18). Turning from being "lovers of pleasures more than lovers of God," the godly conversation confesses, "What seemeth you best I will do," humbling themselves to increase the presence of the Bible's *Mind* in their lives (2 Timothy 3:4, 2 Samuel 18:4, John 3:30). Such souls become "a lover of hospitality, a lover of good men, sober, just, holy, temperate," instructed by that *Spirit* to develop its character (Titus 1:8). By diligently heeding to mediation of this *Spirit's* nature over the organs of our faith, the honest conversation exchanges disobedience for reverence, purifying its heart through faith in the atonement experienced when experimenting with the Bible's words (Proverbs 10:17).

4. Cruelty to the flesh (cruelty to the body of our belief) is not the reformer's lot; instead, they are counseled to "worship God in the spirit, and rejoice in Christ Jesus, and

have no confidence in the flesh" (Philippians 3:3). The living God's chief apostle exposed the definition of sin through his suffering and death, enables discerning conversations to become "the righteousness of God in him" through the wisdom of his act (2 Corinthians 5:21). This wisdom grants the conversation a newly formed character, allowing it to conquer its self for the betterment of the human attached to it (James 1:4, Proverbs 11:5). Trusting in the correctness of the Bible's words, these conversations are perfected by the character of its consolation, for "their righteousness is of me, saith the LORD" (Isaiah 54:17, 1 John 3:24).

5. This "righteousness," an inheritance through faith in the work of the Bible's words upon the personal and the devotional self, is the "holy Spirit of promise," the earnest of our reward for trusting the Bible (Ephesians 1:11, 1:13-14). Without this promise of newness, no fruit of life within the belief grows, for "fools die for want of wisdom" when idols govern the heart (Proverbs 10:21). Yet, "he is in the way of life that keepeth instruction," for "reproofs of instruction are the way of life" (Proverbs 10:17, 6:23). Rejecting the Bible's counsel, hating its wisdom, is to love the death of the conversation's consciousness, but its counsels, being spiritual, quicken the inward parts to enjoy the intended experience of devotional reformation (Proverbs 8:36, Romans 7:14, John 6:63; Proverbs 11:23).

6. An experimental faith with the Bible's words teaches us that "understanding is a wellspring of life unto him that hath it" (Proverbs 16:22). The intended manner of birth, according to the Bible's mind, is through understanding. The devotional conversation's birth is on the Bible's mind, and the conversation conceived through its words learns how to keep their self for right use. (1 John 5:18, 3:9). Instead of chasing what we perceive to be a "Bible belief," instead

of chasing what we take to acceptable "Bible practice," our faith is responsible for its intellect (Proverbs 2:3, 4:5). Like rain watering the earth, the Bible's words are to nourish the seed of faith, producing confidence in its will for our belief (Isaiah 55:10, Hebrews 4:12).

7. Our conversation, that it may eventually become useful, is to be sanctified, or set apart and regenerated, by wisdom (2 Thessalonians 2:13, Philippians 4:17). Wisdom turns the heart from self-sufficiency; this is why "reproofs of instruction are the way of life" (Proverbs 6:23). If we are looking for the right way to carry our belief, the Bible advertises wisdom as a credible vehicle. Written on the heart's tablet, wisdom overcomes pride through patient well-doing, which is why "the patient in spirit is better than the proud in spirit" (Proverbs 3:3, Ecclesiastes 7:8, Romans 2:7). Without devotional correction, the conversation languishes, but the Bible's *medicine* heals; "the LORD will not suffer the soul of the righteous to famish" (Proverbs 10:3).

8. A personal devotion, rooted in the uprightness of the Bible's intention, orders the conversation through wisdom and grace (1 Timothy 2:2). Intemperance, clinging to religious stimulus, rejects the form of love given through the Bible's words, embracing the *serpent's* philosophy of government my religious law (2 Corinthians 11:4). By refusing the instruction of the Bible's *Mind*, we slight its authority, but through the intention of its will for our belief, the heart is perfected in love (2 Thessalonians 3:5). Submitting to its wisdom, the reformed conversation lives honest, humbling its self, bearing the marks of the Bible's kind character in a transformed life (1 Timothy 2:2, 2 Samuel 6:22).

11

Perfect and Entire, Wanting Nothing

1. To walk through life's trials with joy is no small thing; it's a quiet strength, a choice to see hardship not as a curse but as a forge for the soul. When troubles come, whether from within or without, they test our faith, shaping patience that leads to a kind of wholeness nothing else can give (James 1:2-4). Patience, when given room to work, doesn't just steady us, it completes us, leaving no part of our character untouched, no need unmet. This is about embracing and not avoiding pain, knowing that each struggle refines us, strengthens our trust in the Bible's Mind, and proves our hope real before its character (1 John 3:19). Through these moments, we learn by doing, our hearts growing surer as we say with confidence, "I've seen this through" (2 Timothy 4:5; Genesis 30:27).

2. Patience isn't born in comfort, it grows in the heat of tribulation, where faith holds fast and endurance takes root (Romans 5:3-4). Faith itself sparks patience, kindling a fire

that burns through self-doubt and distraction (James 1:3). To restrain our impulses, to tame the hunger for quick relief, is to walk the path of godliness. The one who masters their desires masters their whole being, not by force but by faith in the power of the Bible's words working within (James 3:2). Temperance builds patience, and patience leans on faith; a cycle that strengthens us to face any storm. Without this, we're left to our own frail efforts, but with it, we become whole, our trust in the living God unshaken, our character forged in through the *voice* of the Bible's truth (James 1:4).

3. Trials press us to grow, demanding faith to meet them head-on. Without faith, we falter, relying on our own shaky strength, and the heart turns inward, crafting its own flawed answers (James 1:4). But when faith steps into the fray, patience blooms, perfecting us, and not in pride, but in a quiet reliance on an *Intelligent* hand. Growth doesn't come from ease; it's carved out in struggle, where the heart learns to love what's true, to act with a clear conscience, and to trust without pretense (1 Timothy 1:5). This is the work of the Bible's digested character, shaping us to be complete, lacking nothing, ready for whatever lies ahead (James 1:4).

4. To be "wanting" is to chase shadows, to let the cravings of our *body* of belief lead us astray into religious chaos (2 Peter 2:18). The heart that wanders here is crooked, trapped by its own lies, unable to find the way out (Ecclesiastes 1:15; Isaiah 44:20). It's a path hemmed in by deception, where every step pulls us further from the Bible's *voice* (Lamentations 3:9, 11). Those caught in this spiral see error as unstoppable, their eyes blind to the truth that a right mind is the living God's gift (2 Peter 2:14; 1 John 3:6). They're filled with what fades, with error that chokes out life, no different from ungodliness itself (Romans 1:29; 1 John 3:10). But patience stops this drift, turning us from holding truth captive to living

it freely, opening our hearts to know both ourselves and the Bible's impression (Romans 1:18).

5. Patience begins with restraint, with choosing strength over indulgence, *eating* for life and not for excess (Ecclesiastes 10:17; James 1:4). The conversation's pull must weaken, starved of its old fuel, so the soul of our belief can thrive (3 John 1:2). A disciplined devotional life—watching what feeds our minds—prepares us for the world's unpredictability. Without this, we're unready, tossed by every whim. But through steady faith, guided by the Bible's wisdom, we grow strong, our inner life mirroring the health we show outwardly (James 1:4). This is no private victory; it equips us to face the world, whole in spirit and in purpose.

6. Wholeness comes through sanctification, a work of peace that touches every part of us (1 Thessalonians 5:23). It's not a sudden leap but a patient walk, listening to the Bible's counsel, obeying its truth, and letting it purify us (1 Peter 1:22). Through this, we hold fast to hope in the living God's chief apostle, living by his faith, not our own (1 Peter 1:2; Galatians 2:20). The presence of this counsel in us is the promise of glory, but only if we let his life shape ours, trusting his power to carry us through (Colossians 1:27). Without this surrender, we can't grasp the mystery of its brilliance, or the truth that transforms our devotional experience into something *holy* (Colossians 4:3).

7. Godliness isn't cheap; it costs everything. Conversations seeking it will face resistance, not just from the world but from within (2 Timothy 3:12). Patience grows in this tension, watered by trials and warmed by faith's steady light (Hebrews 12:10). To shy away is to miss the blessing, to refuse the plow of discipline that makes us fruitful (James 1:3; James 2:26). Through confusion and struggle, we learn to listen, to say with courage, "I've followed your *voice*, even

when it led me through danger" (1 Samuel 28:21; Hebrews 12:25). A heart stilled by faith earns *life's* crown, perfected not by ease but by standing firm in hardship (Romans 12:12).

8. This perfection is no shallow thing; it's a deep hope, a longing to reflect the likeness of the Bible's Mind (Romans 8:29). Trials aren't random; they're appointed, shaping us to stand unmoved, knowing we were made for this (1 Thessalonians 3:3). To live godly is to invite correction, to let the living God's will refine us, even when it stings (2 Timothy 3:12). The heart that seeks this lets go of old *idols*, unlearning what's false to embrace what's true, settling into a confidence built on knowing the Mind of the living God directly (1 Peter 4:19). Without humility, faith falters, but with it, the strength of the Bible's mind fills our weakness, making us whole.

9. Patience thrives on a diet of reality, on words that nourish and sustain (1 Timothy 6:3). As we guard our hearts, testing every thought against the Bible's counsel, we shed instability for its manner of righteousness, becoming new in its image (Hebrews 12:9; Ephesians 4:24). This is learned through doing, through trials that teach us to say, "I know this now because I've lived it" (Genesis 30:27). Affliction purges what's false, like fire refining gold, burning away what doesn't belong (Proverbs 17:3; Revelation 3:18). If we dodge this process, we lose the chance to be vessels of honor that are shaped for use (Proverbs 25:4; 1 John 2:29).

10. The living God's chief apostle himself was perfected through suffering, learning obedience in tears, setting the path to follow (Hebrews 5:7-8; John 17:19). He kept his Father's word, sanctifying himself so we might do the same, holding the truth of the scriptures in our hearts (John 8:55; 1 Peter 3:15). His glory is ours to share, but only through the same refining fire, the same surrender to the Bible's Spirit (2 Thessalonians 1:10). This is how we grow complete, through

obedience that shapes every action, blameless before the throne of the Bible's character.

11. Contentment paired with godliness is a treasure, born from a heart that rests in the will of the Bible's wisdom, no matter the storm (1 Timothy 6:6). A meek and quiet spirit, precious to that wisdom, grows here, teaching us to say, "I'm at peace, wherever I am" (1 Peter 3:4; Philippians 4:11). Trials reveal this beauty, a miracle of losing self to find it anew in the gift of resurrection through that wisdom. Patience bears fruit from these scars, watered by mercy, reviving the soul with humility and trust. The heart that yields to this becomes perfect and entire, wanting nothing, alive with that wisdom's unending grace (James 1:4).

12

Established by Righteousness

1. To be rooted in righteousness is to let the heart be shaped by the Mind within the Bible's words, not merely in name, but in the quiet depths where true change begins. It's a circumcision not of the *body* but of the character, a softening of stubborn will, a turning toward those words with open hands and humbled mind (Romans 2:29; Deuteronomy 10:16). The call is clear: break up the hard ground of your heart, clear away the thorns of pride and distraction, and dedicate yourself wholly to understanding within the scriptures (Jeremiah 4:3-4). Cast aside what devotionally defiles, and you'll find a home in the presence of counsel, unshaken by the pull of old ways (Jeremiah 4:1). Once, we let ourselves serve what ruined *us*; chasing one wrong after another; but now, we're urged to offer every part of ourselves to be right, to grow in *holiness* that reflects the heart of the Bible's intention (Romans 6:19).

2. This work starts within, where the Bible stirs the mind to question its habits and desires. It's a call to blunt the sharp edges of our inherited devotional nature, to weaken the grip

of selfish devotional impulses that cloud our spiritual under-standing (Romans 7:14, 18). We're not asked to destroy ourselves but to reshape what drives us, to let go of the old ways that falsely defined the body of our belief (Ephe-sians 4:22). This is more of a deliberate act than a gentle nudge, a grieving of the mind as it wrestles with its own flaws, choosing to stand firm against the demands of the devotional conversation (Genesis 26:35). The Bible urges us to break ground, to cut away what's unyielding, to yield ourselves to a new master—righteousness that leads to wellbeing (Romans 6:19; Daniel 4:27).

3. This struggle is the conversation's constant companion, a battle that doesn't fade as long as we walk in this *body* of faith. The flesh pulls one way, the Bible's Mind another, and we're caught in the tension, learning to master ourselves with honor and purity (1 Thessalonians 4:4). The living God's chief apostle loved what was right and despised what was wrong, and because of this, his mindset stood as a beacon of righteousness, radiant with glory (Hebrews 1:8-9; 2 Corin-thians 3:9). We're called to follow this model, not to mimic outwardly, but to let righteousness reshape us from within, breaking the hold of devotional error through choices that align with the will of the Bible's wisdom (Daniel 4:27).

4. Religious error clings to us naturally, its taste familiar and deceptively sweet. Left to ourselves, we'd never break free; our hearts lean toward what's easy, not what's true (Romans 7:15). The flesh's rule is a kind of death, condemning us to repeat what we know we should hate (2 Corinthians 3:7, 9). But when we turn to righteousness, yielding to its disci-pline, the Bible's Spirit breathes life into our minds, building us into a holy dwelling for the presence of its Mind (1 Peter 2:5). Grace flows freely then, not as a reward, but as a gift

that steadies our steps, pouring from a throne that is both just and merciful (Psalm 45:2; Hebrews 4:16).

5. Righteousness isn't a vague ideal; it's the Bible's counsel given to guide and purify our personal and devotional self (Psalm 119:172, 142, 151). To walk in them is to clear the conscience of lifeless deeds, to serve that counsel with a heart made clean (Hebrews 9:14). It's a philosophical *law* that lights the way of practical devotion, crowning those who follow with wisdom and honor, marking them as its own (Proverbs 8:20; 4:9; Ephesians 1:6). Conversations who live this way show they belong to its character, while conversations turning from righteousness reveal a different allegiance (1 John 3:10; 2:29).

6. This new birth occurs when we take hold of the Bible's words, not just hearing it, but letting it work in us (1 John 1:1). Its voice carries power, even like as the same force that shaped the earth and holds it steady (Jeremiah 10:12; Isaiah 48:13). When we act on its promises, that power strengthens us, perfecting our weakness, proving that grace is enough (2 Corinthians 12:9). It's the same might that created all things, now recreating us, renewing our minds to reflect the One who made *us* (Colossians 1:11, 16; 3:10). Our conversation is blessed by its faith in the power of this manner of creation; not as a prize we earn, but as a gift that makes our conversation right in the living God's sight (Ephesians 2:8; 2 Corinthians 5:21).

7. To grow in godliness is to exercise this faith, to handle the Bible's words with care and let it shape every thought (1 Timothy 4:7). There's no reason to stray from its purpose, no gain in wandering from the mystery of its will (Ephesians 1:9). Victory comes through persistence, through grieving over our shortcomings and choosing righteousness (an active mind to exercise right devotional philosophy) again and

again (Colossians 3:10; 1 John 1:1). Yield to this manner of holiness and the Bible's Mind will guide you into a life that honors its character, marked by reverence and awe (Romans 6:19; Hebrews 12:28).

8. Grace fuels this journey, flowing from a throne that rewards those who seek it (James 1:25). But without effort, without applying our hearts to wisdom, hiding the Bible's commandments within, and guarding them fiercely, we'll miss the call to change (Proverbs 2:1-2; 7:2; Jeremiah 7:5). Ignorance destroys, not because *God* wills it, but because we forget who *He* is, letting our own desires shape us instead (Hosea 4:6; Proverbs 19:2). When we pause to examine our ways, to question the fruit of our choices, shame can lead us back to truth, reminding us of the advocate we have in the Bible's philosophy (Romans 6:21; 1 John 2:1).

9. Faith isn't real unless it's lived, unless we keep the Bible's commandments with a heart that knows them (1 John 2:3). Without surrender, we'll twist its character to fit our own ideas, missing its grace entirely (Ephesians 1:20). Our Father has given a light of philosophy to guide our belief, to preserve us not just from error but also for devotional holiness (Ephesians 1:22; 3:15). The counsel is simple: break free by choosing righteousness, by examining what feeds our soul and rejecting what poisons it (Daniel 4:27; 1 Corinthians 6:19).

10. We don't own our devotional self; understanding holds the keys to its life and death (Psalm 68:20). Through the Bible's counsel we put to death what drags our belief down, finding life in obedience to its philosophy (Romans 8:13). Its manner of love fills us, but only if we let our hearts be cut and shaped by it (Romans 5:5). This means silencing the mind's proud thoughts, capturing every impulse to serve its revelation (2 Corinthians 10:5). It's a high calling, a pressing

toward a prize that demands everything (Philippians 3:14). Its Spirit convicts, guarding us from devotional condemnation, offering freedom where guilt once ruled (John 16:8; Romans 5:9-10; 1 Corinthians 11:32; 2 Corinthians 3:17).

13

The Essence of Godly Living

1. The heart of godly living beats quietly, not in loud displays or mindless passions, but in the steady rhythm of a spirit that seeks wisdom's presence. It's found in the hidden places of the soul, where a meek and quiet spirit grows, an ornament that doesn't fade, cherished deeply by the One who sees all (1 Peter 3:4). This is the life our devotional conversation is called to: judged by the world's harsh measures, yet alive in the Bible's Spirit, shaped by its fact (1 Peter 4:6). To live this way is to root ourselves in its mercy, which holds us steady like a sheltering hand, promising peace that overflows and grace that will never run dry (1 Peter 1:3).

2. Conversations embracing this gift of right-mindedness find themselves walking a path of faith, love, and holiness, anchored in clarity of purpose (Romans 5:17; 1 Timothy 2:15). They are called to live as not chasing approval, but as resting in the peace that comes from trusting the Bible's boundless wisdom (1 Thessalonians 2:12; Romans 5:1). This peace isn't earned through religious *perfection* but through a faith that dares to act, that leans into the Bible's riches; not

the kind that rusts, but the enduring wealth of its counsel (Psalm 52:7; Proverbs 8:18). To live according to the living God in the Spirit means standing before the religious world's judgment; its quick glances and shallow measures; while choosing a deeper mindful and philosophical life, where the Bible's truth reigns (1 Peter 4:6).

3. The religious world judges by what it sees, as when the living God's chief apostle faced a crowd ready to condemn a woman caught in *error*. He saw beyond their accusations, pointing out that human eyes cling to surfaces (John 8:15; 1 Samuel 16:7). The living God's judgment, though, cuts to the heart, grounded in a philosophical law that leads to reality (Romans 2:2; Psalm 119:142). Conversations claiming godliness will face scrutiny, not just from others but also from this philosophical law's mirror, showing where they've strayed (Romans 2:12). The world may mock a life that doesn't chase its excesses, sneering at those who choose restraint over riotous spiritual indulgence (1 Peter 4:4). Yet the Bible's will is clear: to bear this criticism with a steady conscience, even when it stings unjustly, is to grow stronger in the Mind of its character (1 Peter 2:19).

4. Living godly means facing a tug-of-war between two ways of being. The body of our belief naturally pulls toward excess, craving religious opulence, revelry, or idols that promise joy but deliver only chains (1 Peter 4:3). It revels in chaos, calling it freedom, blind to the truth that chasing pleasure without purpose is a kind of death (2 Peter 2:13; 1 Timothy 5:6). The Bible's wisdom, though, offers a different center, a renewing of the mind that lifts us above lame desires (Ephesians 4:23). As we turn from indulgence, devotional health begins to bloom, like rain softening parched ground. The world around us tests this choice, pressing us to conform, but through these trials, we learn to live according

to the living God in the spirit of our mind, letting the Bible's *voice* guide our steps (1 Peter 4:6).

5. The Bible's philosophy reaches even those dead in their devotional ways, for a mind set on the body of its belief is death itself, unable to bend to the law of the Bible's philosophy (1 Peter 4:6; Romans 8:6-7). It clings to what's *cursed*, like a tree marked for ruin (Deuteronomy 21:23). But conversations chosen to transcend, awakened by the Bible's sanctifying touch, find life in unexpected places (1 Peter 1:2). The Bible's law of life reveals our flaws, showing us our need for grace (Romans 7:10). Criticism from those who don't carry this law in their hearts becomes a tool, refining us to serve its principles more fully (Galatians 6:2). Through our struggle the living God breathes life into our mortal devotional frames, urging us to walk in newness, not clinging to old religious habits but stepping boldly into our faith's purpose (Romans 8:11; 6:4).

6. To live godly is to invite persecution, not as a curse, but as a forge where faith is shaped (2 Timothy 3:12). Godliness grows through wisdom, restraint, and patience, perfected in quiet devotion to the Bible's logic. This faith isn't private; it spills into public life, drawing both scorn and wonder. The Bible's law becomes a joy to those who love it, a guide they study with delight, eager to live out their Father's will (Romans 7:22). Their lives reflect an inner truth, a hidden strength that shines through their actions (1 Peter 3:4).

7. The religious world, lost in its own noise, may not see this. Minds clouded by vanity and ignorance turn away from this manner of life, blind to the light of a simple and mindful living experience (Ephesians 4:17-18). Yet the godly conversation endures, finding joy in suffering for what's right, counting it a privilege to bear shame (1 Peter 2:20; Acts 5:41). When reproached, such a conversation doesn't

shrink back; it rejoices. The Bible's Spirit rests on them, a glory that outweighs any scorn (1 Peter 4:14). Their contentment lies in keeping its law, knowing that each trial carves its truth deeper into their hearts (Proverbs 29:18). Even as others speak ill of their faith's character, their lives glorify the Bible's wisdom, sometimes stirring a spark of longing in those who watch (1 Peter 4:14).

8. Godliness isn't a solitary path; it binds us to others, calling us to share in wisdom's struggles (2 Timothy 1:8). Our conversation is called to this, to carry the weight of love even when it costs us (1 Peter 2:21). A meek and quiet spirit, so precious to the living God, pairs with grace's crown, a mark of glory that sets the godly conversation apart (1 Peter 3:4; Proverbs 4:9). They press forward, undeterred by scars, bearing their scars with resolve (Philippians 3:14; Galatians 6:17). Unlike those who dodge suffering to avoid the weight of their conscience, the godly conversation stands firm, their presence a quiet testimony to a life lived for understanding (Galatians 6:12; 1 Peter 4:6).

9. Once, they too wandered; foolish, lost in spiritual lusts and religious malice, like so many others (Titus 3:3). But mercy found them, abundant grace washing away unbelief with faith and love (1 Timothy 1:13-14). Now they live to proclaim that the Bible's wisdom heals, pouring themselves out for others, even when love isn't returned (1 Timothy 1:15; 2 Corinthians 12:15). They've entrusted their souls to its wellspring, enduring hardship not for pride, but for the sake of that wisdom's will, knowing it is faithful (1 Peter 4:19). This choice sets a line: no longer living for damaging desires, but for their devotional purpose alone (1 Peter 4:2).

10. Suffering, whether from within or without, has a purpose. To the hungry soul, even bitterness tastes sweet, for it leads to truth (Proverbs 27:7). The godly conversation

counts all else as loss, longing only for the breath offered through enduring (Philippians 3:8; Psalm 73:25). Faith speaks boldly here, calling us to stand alone with counsel, revived by its blessings and driven to serve others (Romans 10:6; Isaiah 51:2; 1 Corinthians 9:19). Trials, whether self-examination or the world's pressures, reveal our flaws, not to break us, but to show us where the living God's hand can work. Denying the urges of our *body* of belief builds wisdom, letting the intelligence shape a heart that reflects the love at the center of the scriptures.

11. True godliness doesn't spring from empty words or hollow gestures. The living God sees when lips praise but hearts drift far (Isaiah 29:13). Real faith lives in the spirit of the conversation's conscience, carried out through a mind renewed daily (Ephesians 4:23; Romans 12:2). This renewal brings clarity, a sobriety that mirrors the faith of wisdom's family (1 Corinthians 4:6; 2 Peter 1:1; Acts 24:24-25). Conversations seeking this faith bring their whole selves into submission, not chasing forms or titles, but honoring the Bible's Mind in truth and action (1 John 3:18).

12. This path demands courage, courage to face hardship like a soldier, to hold fast to what's true (2 Timothy 2:3; 3:14). It assures the heart before the living God, not with arrogance, but with a longing to be whole, to reflect the perfection of the Bible's character (1 John 3:19). Good works flow naturally from this, not as a show, but as love spilling over, eager to lift others up (Titus 2:14; Romans 15:2). Godliness isn't random, it's deliberate, built on a virtue guiding us to live wisely in the sight of the Bible's philosophy.

13. To live according to God in the spirit of our mind is to let the Bible's manner of love shape every thought, every deed (1 Peter 4:6). It's a life of purpose, not perfection, where faith grows through trials, and wisdom blooms

in surrender. The godly conversation doesn't just endure, it thrives, its hearts alive with a certain fire for understanding, its life a testament to the unending grace that is found within wisdom.

14

According to God in the Spirit

1. To live according to the living God in the spirit of the mind is to step into a devotional life reshaped by purpose, where the heart and mind are gently but firmly molded to reflect something greater than oneself. It's a call to transformation, not through force, but through a quiet renewal of thought and intention, so we might come to know what is good, acceptable, and perfectly aligned with the will at the center of the Bible (Romans 12:2). This isn't about chasing rules for one's own sake; it's about letting the Bible's Mind guide us toward a life where our choices echo its manner of love. When we hold fast to its counsel, we find that love taking root deep within, growing complete and whole (1 John 2:5). For the student of the Bible, this means carrying the name of the Bible's philosophy, not just in words, but in the way we live, with a character shaped by its character, proving we truly know its Mind by keeping its instruction (1 John 2:3).

2. The Bible's instruction is the heartbeat of its truth. To walk in this truth is to possess a purified devotional character,

to let its wisdom cleanse us from within. But purity doesn't come without struggle. To live without inner conflict is to risk stagnation, to let corruption settle within our inward person. Those conversations claiming to know *God* yet bear no demonstrative fruit from that relationship; those conversations that haven't first admitted their own losses; miss the chance to speak the Bible's hidden wisdom (Philippians 3:8; 1 Corinthians 2:7). Their words, along with their experience, will ring hollow, for they lack the marks of a life surrendered to transformation.

3. What does the Bible's Spirit teach us? It points to our spiritual blindness, gently but firmly showing that clinging to our own understanding keeps us bound to religious error (John 9:41). When we pretend our flawed human insight is enough, we turn away from the reality offered through the Bible's philosophy. To deny that truth is to call the Bible's *voice* a liar, to lean on the shaky ground of our own hearts instead of its steady wisdom (1 John 5:10). We are therefore reminded that we deceive ourselves when claiming we're free of error only; truth can't take root where honesty falters (1 John 1:8). Our hearts, left unchecked, are tangled in mindless personal and devotional desires, built on what fades away (1 Peter 3:21). But those who follow the Bible's intention speak a different wisdom, not the kind that crumbles with the world, but one taught through the inspiration of the Bible's wisdom (1 Corinthians 2:6, 13).

4. Many stumble here, clinging to old religious ways or empty spiritual rituals, mistaking them for truth (Colossians 2:14). They drift into error, rejecting the love of understanding for something less (2 Thessalonians 2:10; 1 John 4:6). But conversations embracing the Bible's *voice* receive its guiding influence, a gift for those who believe in and experiment with the power of its words (John 7:39). The point is to

have to law of the Bible's philosophy written onto our hearts. Without this law etched in our hearts, we fail to honor the Bible's intention for our character (2 Corinthians 3:3). We need to exercise faith in the power of that law to resurrect our character when on this journey; it's in remembering our missteps, in feeling the weight of our errors, that we learn how to live differently (Ezekiel 36:31; 11:19). This is how we grow to live according to the living God in the spirit of our mind, even through an honest reckoning that reshapes us (1 Peter 4:6).

5. The Spirit's command shines a light on our shortcomings, not to condemn, but to reveal the true weight of religious error, making it undeniable (Romans 7:13). It draws us to the goodness at the Bible's center, showing us our hunger for what's lasting and true. We owe nothing to our old religious ways; the Bible desires every conversation to understand the reality regarding the condition of their devotional character, to live in a way that reflects its manner of well-being (Romans 8:12; 1 Timothy 2:4; Titus 1:1).

6. A mind rooted in the Bible's manner of love brings life and peace, because the Bible's Spirit itself is life, born of a right will for our human and spiritual being (Romans 8:6, 10). To live by that influence of truth is to let our thoughts and actions align with its will (John 15:26; 1 John 4:6). It's a daily choice to let its truth guide our devotional journey, keeping us from straying. Without this, we risk falling back into old spiritual patterns, shaped by deceitful religious desires (Ephesians 2:3; 4:22). But in the sphere of the Bible's counsel, we're remade, created anew in its right will, free to honor the living God in truth and in understanding (Ephesians 4:24; John 4:23).

7. "Righteousness" isn't just a word; it's the fruit of doing the Bible's will, proof we're born of its character (1

John 2:29). Its words, living and life-giving, gives our conversation life, and by learning of and doing its will, our faith's conscience forever exists undisturbed (1 Peter 1:23; 1 John 2:17). This is the path to a full life, where wisdom multiplies our belief's days and grace strengthens our devotion (Proverbs 3:2; 9:11; 2 Peter 1:2). Those who seek this will find the Bible's wisdom, not one of fear or bondage, but of power, love, and clarity (John 7:17; 2 Timothy 1:7; Romans 8:15). A sound heart, grounded in fact, becomes the life of the whole body of belief (Proverbs 14:30; Titus 2:10).

8. The Bible's philosophy breathes life into every mind interacting with it, and just as the living God's chief apostle was raised by that same *Spirit*, so we're called to walk in newness of devotional life, bearing *fruit* that lasts (1 Timothy 6:13; 1 Peter 3:18; Romans 6:4; 7:4). Religious error pulls our conversation toward *death*, but grace makes us servants of righteousness or of doing the right will, living from a pure heart and genuine faith (Romans 7:5; 6:18; 1 Timothy 1:5). Through the Bible's Mind, we're transformed, our minds renewed as we weigh spiritual truths together, letting our hearts search for wisdom (1 Corinthians 2:13).

9. So, live according to the living God, through the Bible's influence, in the spirit of your mind (1 Peter 4:6). Let its words quicken you, as it did the living God's chief apostle (Psalm 119:154; 1 Peter 3:18). This path isn't easy; our example's heart was broken by reproach, and to the point where he, for the sake of the philosophy that he spoke, had to humble himself to death (Psalm 69:20; Philippians 2:8). Like him, our conversation will also face trials, but through them all, it will be refined (Acts 14:22).

10. If we shy away from this struggle, if we hide from the manner of faith that living God's chief apostle demonstrated, we risk being turned away from an experience with

the Bible's *light* (2 Timothy 2:12). His life was marked by a philosophical sorrow, yet his conversation fulfilled the Bible's will so we might know the purpose attached to our own (Isaiah 53:3; Job 22:21). He was among few that knew and then taught about the refreshing influence at the center of the scriptures, and it is his conversation that promises not to leave our conversation comfortless (John 14:18). His obedience purified his belief, and it is by joining into his conversation's experience that we find our belief also purified (John 15:3; 17:19).

11. The living God's chief apostle came to do the will at the center of the scriptures, and the living God works in us to do the same, shaping our conversation to vessels of a rare wisdom in love (John 6:38; Philippians 2:13; Ephesians 1:4). As we follow the Bible's *voice*, its Mind fuels our every step, keeping our belief in its right will. Without this constant renewal, we drift, but under its guidance, we find life, free from *death's* grip, just as our example's devotional conversation lives unto our Father forever (2 Thessalonians 2:13; Romans 6:9-10). Live, then, according to the living God in the spirit of your mind, and let fact make your belief whole (1 Peter 4:6).

15

Shall Live Through Him

1. Let us begin with a foundational assertion: the conversation publicly affirming that the living God's chief apostle possessed an anointed conversation enters into a relationship with that conversation's anointing (1 John 4:15). This is not a casual acknowledgment, but a sure mental commitment, one that leads to a transformative experience where the Bible's wisdom, as seed, takes root and persists, rendering devotional error an untenable contradiction within such a life (1 John 3:9; Luke 8:11). Consider the implications: those conversations conceived by that wisdom exhibit its *righteousness* not as an accessory, but as an intrinsic quality, a condition wherein *sin*, because that wisdom is active, finds no place (1 John 2:29; 1 John 5:18).

2. Now, let's extend this inquiry: every conversation enacting *righteousness* is, by definition, born of the Bible, for what originates from its words overcomes the *world* (1 John 2:29; 1 John 5:4). The "world" here is not in reference to the literal world, but to the religious world and its appetites (1 John 2:16; Ephesians 2:2). In response to the consciousness

within the religious word, we have the influence and the philosophical example of the living God's chief apostle (1 John
4:14). To confess this minister's conversation as the living
God's intended guide is to align oneself with a life lived
through his ministry's wisdom, putting away the flesh-based
pursuits of the devotional conversation for the living God's
enduring will of God (1 John 4:9; 1 Peter 4:2). To the Bible's
mind, it is not ultimately the person that triumphs, but rather
the conversation that is born from out of an interaction with
the Bible's words (1 John 5:4; 1 John 4:6; Ephesians 2:2).
This distinction invites us to think on the locus of agency: is
it the individual, or the living principle of the Bible's words
within the individual, that effects this overcoming?

3. This experience transcends the traditional religious
experience when next understanding that those who love
are born of the living God because the living God is ultimately *love*, which experience is not without life-altering
ramifications (1 John 4:7-8). This *love* was found within the
living God's chief apostle and manifested through his willing
sacrifice, a demonstration of an intelligent affection amidst
apparent human failure (1 John 4:10; Romans 5:8). To know
the living God, then, is to embody this love and its wisdom,
which knowledge is authenticated by a relationship with the
living God's commandments (1 John 2:3). Here we encounter
an interesting formula where love and right action constitute
the victory that extricates the conversation from the religious
world's spiritual distortions, anchoring the devotional self in
a truth emanating from the living God's *Mind* (1 John 2:16;
Isaiah 51:4).

4. This is the Bible's framework for understanding how
to perfect and reform our personal devotional conversation.
Yet consider next the commandments, which are unequivo-
cally for our belief's wellbeing (Psalm 119:172). When the

mind is informed by the Bible and purified by its discipline *sin*, due to the seed of the Bible's wisdom resting within, becomes an enduring impossibility (1 Peter 1:23; Ephesians 5:26; 1 John 3:9; Luke 8:11). What is born of the Bible's words—the Bible's philosophy—prevails over the religious world, silencing the cacophony of self-justification known to the religious milieu and offering a faith that dismantles the structure of *sin* (1 John 5:4; Romans 3:19; Romans 6:6). This is a call to intellectual and moral discipline: to confess this truth is to mute one's own rationalizations, embracing a faith that reconfigures the devotional self in alignment with the Bible's intention.

5. This reconfiguration finds its mechanism in the "law of the Spirit of life" (Romans 8:2), which liberates by virtue of the condemnation of the religious world given by the living God's chief apostle's (John 8:23). His mission, we are told, was to declare the living God's *name*; a revelation sustained by fidelity to commandments that articulate the living God's devotional character (John 17:26). To live through the living God's chief apostle is to internalize the wisdom surrounding his ministry, accessing a mindset defining the Bible's will and spiritual economy (1 John 4:9; John 6:63; 1 Corinthians 1:24, 30). Knowledge of him, however, requires a rigorous self-mastery, subduing the body of belief to love and obey the Bible's perception, highlighting the interplay between volition and destined encounter (1 Corinthians 9:27; Philippians 3:10; 1 John 4:7; 1 John 2:3).

6. The commandments of the living God and the faith of the living God's chief apostle are inseparable, a unity ordained to redeem the religious world through their wisdom (Colossians 4:3). To speak "truth" is to manifest right Bible understanding, for the law of the Bible's conscience is truth, and confessing the living God's man reveals the mystery of

the Bible's godliness, which is right devotional wisdom within a devotional body initially conceived *dead* (Psalm 119:142; 1 Timothy 3:16). This godliness emerges as the living God's voice figuratively assumes *flesh*, the Bible's words shaping the body of our understanding to become our belief's ultimate covering. (John 1:14; Romans 8:3; Hebrews 5:8). To know the living God is to live the Bible's commandments, a life distinct from a religious world that neither comprehends nor embraces them (1 John 3:1, 13). This separation is necessary for a re-orientation of devotional identity.

7. Thus, our devotional conversation is summoned from the religious world, like the living God's chief apostle, to live through the enduring legacy of his devotional character by mirroring his reverence for the scriptures (John 17:16; 1 John 4:9). This entails a bold pursuit of the Bible's mind, a devotional life conformed to the death and resurrection of his belief (Exodus 33:18; Philippians 3:10). Such an experience, illuminated by the Bible's wisdom, squashes the nature of *sin*, curbing the appetite to preserve spiritual vitality (Romans 3:20; Proverbs 23:2; Romans 8:10). Philosophically, this is sanctification, even a renewal of the inner devotional self confessing the sonship of the living God's chief apostle's through our conversation's deportment (Ephesians 3:16; Romans 5:9; 1 Peter 1:22).

8. This journey matures in love and wisdom through adherence to the experience of the living God's chief apostle, a sanctification that rejects the religious world's idolatrous impulses (1 Thessalonians 4:3; 1 John 2:16). The conversation's existence becomes a testament to his love, perfected as his mindset indwells, uniting one and with their conversation's conscience to fulfill the Bible's inward purpose (John 17:23; 1 John 3:24). This is then the reformer's charge: to live by the Bible's *Mind*, renewed in knowledge after its wisdom's

image, revitalized by surrender to grace (Colossians 3:10). Absent this, there is no health for the mind or progress in the devotional experience; only an intimate relationship with the can satisfy the type of resurrection the living God intends.

16

By the Spirit of His Chief Apostle

1. "Whosoever believeth that Jesus is the Christ is born of God: and every one that loveth him that begat loveth him also that is begotten of him" (1 John 5:1). Thus it is written, and further declared, "No man hath seen God at any time; the only begotten Son, which is in the bosom of the Father, he hath declared him" (John 1:18). Herein lies the mystery of divine filiation: he who acknowledges the Son acknowledges the Father, and in this sacred bond, love is perfected.

2. Those who repose faith in the name of the living God's chief Apostle—whose name is of God, "who hath reconciled us to himself by Jesus Christ" (2 Corinthians 5:18), "by the death of his Son" (Romans 5:10), "by whom we have now received the atonement" (Romans 5:11), "through faith in his blood" (Romans 3:25)—to them is granted "power to become the sons of God" (John 1:12), that they might "joy in God through our Lord Jesus Christ" (Romans 5:11). They who diligently search and act upon the faith of the living God's chief Apostle are begotten anew by the Word of His Spirit. This regeneration, ordained by the authority

bestowed through the untainted reception of His sacrifice's virtue, endows the believer with wisdom and peace, yea, even praise and reverence unto the Lord through "joy in the Holy Ghost" (Romans 14:17).

3. Should the Bible's student apprehend that the *Word* is *God*, then such a one must receive the power of the *Holy Ghost*, "that he might bring us to God" (1 Peter 3:18). The ministry of the living God's chief apostle was one of reconciliation and restoration unto the likeness of the living God's devotional character; thus, the Spirit's Word is "made unto us wisdom, and righteousness, and sanctification, and redemption" (1 Corinthians 1:30). He who first resolves to believe, through faith in the atonement, uniting his spirit with His Spirit in communion—a communion whereby the believer is "renewed in knowledge after the image of him that created him" (Colossians 3:10)—shall be born of God, "not of blood, nor of the will of the flesh, nor of the will of man, but of God" (John 1:13). For "flesh and blood cannot inherit the kingdom of God" (1 Corinthians 15:50); rather, the soul's reformer must "be born of water and of the Spirit" (John 3:5), that is, "with the washing of water by the word" (Ephesians 5:26).

4. Once more, the mind "who first trusted in Christ" (Ephesians 1:12) is yielded unto the Spirit, to be purified and hallowed "with the washing of water by the word" (Ephesians 5:26). What then is inscribed? "He that saith he abideth in him ought himself also so to walk, even as he walked" (1 John 2:6). "This is he that came by water and blood, even Jesus Christ" (1 John 5:6); hence, the believer is not merely born of water "by the washing of regeneration" (Titus 3:5), but also by "the precious blood of Christ, as of a lamb without blemish and without spot" (1 Peter 1:19). For this cause it is proclaimed, "That which is born of the Spirit

is spirit" (John 3:6), and through the Spirit's discipline, the reformer avows, "I serve with my spirit in the gospel of his Son" (Romans 1:9). By the Spirit's renewal of the mind, "the fruit of the Spirit is in all goodness and righteousness and truth" (Ephesians 5:9).

5. "That the righteousness of the law might be fulfilled in us, who walk not after the flesh, but after the Spirit" (Romans 8:4), the believer is welcomed into "the ministration of the spirit" (2 Corinthians 3:8) and "the ministration of righteousness" (2 Corinthians 3:9). "Christ being come an high priest of good things to come, by a greater and more perfect tabernacle" (Hebrews 9:11), "when he had by himself purged our sins, sat down on the right hand of the Majesty on high" (Hebrews 1:3), "that we might be made the righteousness of God in him" (2 Corinthians 5:21). This ministry of the living God's chief Apostle is appointed to fulfill the decree, "Bind up the testimony, seal the law among my disciples" (Isaiah 8:16). As the believer is renewed and sanctified by enacting the Word of God through faith in the righteousness of the living God's chief Apostle's counsel, it is affirmed, "Every one that doeth righteousness is born of him" (1 John 2:29), "by the Spirit which he hath given us" (1 John 3:24).

6. "Whosoever believeth that Jesus is the Christ is born of God" (1 John 5:1). As many gazed upon Jesus, "looking upon Jesus as he walked" (John 1:36), it was manifest that He was the living God's chief Apostle, for it was revealed, "He that sent me to baptize with water, the same said unto me, Upon whom thou shalt see the Spirit descending, and remaining on him, the same is he which baptizeth with the Holy Ghost" (John 1:33). The living God's chief Apostle walked in the Spirit of His Father, living and laboring thereby; thus it was proclaimed, "Behold the Lamb of God!" (John 1:36). Wherefore, the believer is assured, "He shall

give you another Comforter, that he may abide with you for ever" (John 14:16), "which is the earnest of our inheritance until the redemption of the purchased possession" (Ephesians 1:14). And so, "hereby know we that we dwell in him, and he in us, because he hath given us of his Spirit" (1 John 4:13). As the Spirit abode upon the living God's chief Apostle, sustaining His walk of love and devotion, so too the reformer is exhorted, "Walk in love" (Ephesians 5:2), "because the love of God is shed abroad in our hearts by the Holy Ghost which is given unto us" (Romans 5:5).

7. If there is a profession of confidence in the living God's chief apostle, there must also be a love for the living God. If there should be a dedication to the living God's chief apostle, and a heartfelt gratitude for his willing surrender in defense of the Bible's philosophy, if the one proclaims crucifixion and resurrection by wisdom within that man's surrender, (Galatians 2:20), then it must follow that they are submitted unto the inward education of that act. (Romans 3:22). Should one lack the wisdom of the Bible's intention for the devotional conversation, their profession becomes an idol, "for they being ignorant of God's righteousness, and going about to establish their own righteousness, have not submitted themselves unto the righteousness of God" (Romans 10:3). Thus it is written, "That which is born of the flesh is flesh" (John 3:6), "for if ye live after the flesh, ye shall die" (Romans 8:13).

8. Hence, "if any man have not the Spirit of the living God's chief Apostle, he is none of his" (Romans 8:9). "The Spirit is life because of righteousness" (Romans 8:10), "so then they that are in the flesh cannot please God" (Romans 8:8), for such a mind "is not subject to the law of God, neither indeed can be" (Romans 8:7). The Spirit is of truth, its fruit being "in all goodness and righteousness and truth"

(Ephesians 5:9), and they who yield unto that revelation are submitted to the divine science of devotional creation, honoring the counsel, "Be ye transformed by the renewing of your mind" (Romans 12:2). We know we love the character of the living God because we uphold faith through the virtue of the Bible's words; and by submitting ourselves to the Bible's wisdom, we are assured that the devotional character of the living God's chief apostle shall be inscribed within our devotional conversation's thoughts and feelings, for we are "changed into the same image from glory to glory, even as by the Spirit of the Lord" (2 Corinthians 3:18).

9. It is an established truth that "it is God which worketh in you both to will and to do of his good pleasure" (Philippians 2:13). The living God's chief apostle willing spilt his blood as an example encouraging conversations to separate their minds from the religious world (Hebrews 9:14). The Bible's reformer, by fulfilling the law of its intention, is ordained to "keep his commandments, and do those things that are pleasing in his sight" (1 John 3:22). This obedience is wrought by his mindset resting upon and within their devotional conscience. Possessing a devotional conversation ordained through the Bible's wisdom, his mindset instructs in what is right by the true image thereof, "because the Spirit is truth" (1 John 5:6). "Every one that loveth him that begat loveth him also that is begotten of him" (1 John 5:1); therefore, to love not the living God is to despise the devotional character of his chief witness.

10. They that love the living God shall fall as dead before the revelation of his benevolence; they that cherish his *name* will embrace the education of that benevolence, that it may dwell within their hearts. We know we love not the character of the living God when we harden our hearts against his manner of *love*. We know we love not his *name* when we cease

to trust faithfully in the reconciliation of our inward person unto his *Mind*. If we love the name of is chief witness then, by the commandment of that witness' ministry, our devotional character are perfected into the likeness of his devotional character—that image which reflects the living God, established upon his ten immutable principles of liberty and godly benevolence.

11. If the Bible's student truly loves the Bible's Faith, they will love the heart and foundation of the living God's chief apostle. This man once confessed, "But that the world may know that I love the Father" (John 14:31); how then can one be justified in neglecting the foundation of his profession? Hear a summary of his words: "I will declare thy name unto my brethren" (Hebrews 2:12), and, "Whosoever shall do the will of God, the same is my brother, and my sister, and mother" (Mark 3:35). Thus, it is well said, "This is the will of God, even your sanctification" (1 Thessalonians 4:3), that "the mystery of God, and of the Father, and of Christ" (Colossians 2:2) might be proclaimed by the believer through his chief apostle's *name* and *knowledge*, even as he is said to have affirmed, "I have kept my Father's commandments, and abide in his love" (John 15:10).

12. "If ye keep my commandments, ye shall abide in my love" (John 15:10), counsels our example devotional conversation. Our devotional conversation must be born of the wisdom attached to his ministry, alive unto that wisdom's living God, abiding in the benevolence of that wisdom, and governed by every within the Bible, growing daily in the knowledge of the living God's chief apostle's *name* through learning and exercising those commandments. Hence the warning, "He that loveth me not keepeth not my sayings: and the word which ye hear is not mine, but the Father's which sent me" (John 14:24).

13. "He that hath the Son hath life" (1 John 5:12), and this *life* is granted because "he that is begotten of God keepeth himself" (1 John 5:18) "according to the will of God" (1 Peter 4:19). Thus, the conversation doing *heaven's* Word or Wisdom shall be perfected in love as they "suffer according to the will of God" (1 Peter 4:19), a suffering described as being reproached for the growth and the development of the devotional conversation's character. Such an ordeal engenders godliness within an erring devotional life, imprinting the mind of the living God's chief apostle within the doers conversation (Colossians 1:27); yet the heart must first heed the counsel, "Every one that loveth him that begat loveth him also that is begotten of him" (1 John 5:1).

17

True Living Devotion

1. It is written, "Live according to God in the spirit" (1 Peter 4:6); a pure devotional conversation is not measured by earthly rituals, nor is it confined to the physical form. Rather, it flourishes in the soul's alignment with the Creator, made possible "through the faith of the operation of God" (Colossians 2:12). This is the sacred calling: to keep and honor the commandments of God, not merely in outward observance, but in the very depths of our mind's spirit. This is why it says, "For the letter killeth, but the spirit giveth life" (2 Corinthians 3:6).

2. Thus, the living God's chief apostle declared, "Neither in this mountain, nor yet at Jerusalem, worship the Father" (John 4:21). No mere place is holy in itself, for the true sanctity of worship is found not in a structure of stone, but in a heart fashioned by the living God's hands. "The true worshippers shall worship the Father in spirit and in truth: for the Father seeketh such to worship him" (John 4:23).

3. The true disciple of the Bible does not rest his faith upon the magnificence of a cathedral or the traditions of

men, nor does he trust in the fleeting visions of his own heart. Their devotional conscience testifies, "We know what we worship" (John 4:22), and the faithful speak with conviction, "We speak that we do know, and testify that we have seen" (John 3:11). They proclaim, "That which we have seen and heard declare we unto you" (1 John 1:3). The spirit of the mind is renewed only by one means: "Get wisdom, get understanding" (Proverbs 4:5). And again, "Get wisdom: and with all thy getting get understanding" (Proverbs 4:7). For true knowledge is not abstract theory but the living experience of faith, the tangible encounter with the Bible's words, moving one to confess, "That which we have looked upon, and our hands have handled" (1 John 1:1).

4. To function according to God in the spirit is to embrace his commandments, not as burdens but as the very breath of life. "God is a Spirit" (John 4:24), and therefore, those who seek the living God must come in spiritual sincerity, their minds renewed by discipline, their steps guided by wisdom. "The new man, which is renewed in knowledge" (Colossians 3:10) is one who bears "the image of him that created him" (Colossians 3:10). This renewal is no mere intellectual ascent but an act of inward transformation, for "be ye transformed by the renewing of your mind" (Romans 12:2), and in that transformation, one discerns "what is that good, and acceptable, and perfect, will of God" (Romans 12:2).

5. There is no newness of mind without a severance from the old. No fresh wellspring of love is born where corruption is still cherished. The commandments of God are not cold inscriptions on tablets of stone but living realities, carried out through faith by the operation of the Bible's words. "For by grace are ye saved through faith; and that not of yourselves" (Ephesians 2:8) it says, "not of works" (Ephesians 2:9), but through belief "on him that justifieth the ungodly" (Romans

4:5). And in this sacred reckoning, "faith is counted for righteousness" (Romans 4:5).

6. This righteousness, "the righteousness of God which is by faith" (Romans 3:22), is the garment of the redeemed devotional conversation, woven from the very fabric of obedience. The believer is called to abide in this righteousness, to be "transformed by the renewing of your mind" (Romans 12:2), not through hollow ritual, but through the living proof of obedience. The conversation's spirit flourishes in the doing of the Bible's words, for wisdom is gained not in theory but in the refining fire of practice. "Apply thine heart" (Proverbs 2:2) to the pursuit of truth, and, "Keep my commandments, and live" (Proverbs 7:2), living according to God in the spirit (1 Peter 4:6), for he has promised, "All shall know me" (Hebrews 8:11), and the evidence of "knowing" is this: "Hereby we do know that we know him, if we keep his commandments" (1 John 2:3).

7. "His commandments are not grievous" (1 John 5:3), for the fruit of obedience is love itself, which is "charity out of a pure heart" (1 Timothy 1:5). In this truth is the world divided: "In this the children of God are manifest, and the children of the devil" (1 John 3:10). "He that doeth truth cometh to the light, that his deeds may be made manifest" (John 3:21), for even "the deeds of the body" (Romans 8:13) must testify to the transformation within. "Every one that doeth righteousness is born of him" (1 John 2:29), for by the law is "the knowledge of sin" (Romans 3:20), and through the revelation of that knowledge, the soul is drawn to redemption.

8. The living God's chief apostle, upon the cross, "abolished in his flesh the enmity, even the law of commandments contained in ordinances" (Ephesians 2:15). And this redemption extends "not only in this world, but also in that which

is to come" (Ephesians 1:21). The believer's conversation, through faith, must likewise put to death its "sin," learning correct sorrow and repentance that the devotional body may be moved towards reform. For "every one that doeth evil hateth the light" (John 3:20), refusing the reproof that could save him. Nevertheless "he is in the way of life that keepeth instruction: but he that refuseth reproof erreth" (Proverbs 10:17).

9. True obedience is not servitude; it is the gateway to love and wisdom. "Whoso keepeth his word, in him verily is the love of God perfected" (1 John 2:5). Faith is not a passive state; it is a struggle, a refining fire. The storms of trial will pass, and when they do, the soul will be left "perfect and entire, wanting nothing" (James 1:4).

10. The temple of worship is no longer built by human hands, but within the spirit of the devotional conversation's conscience. which is why it says, "I will put my law in their inward parts, and write it in their hearts" (Jeremiah 31:33). Thus, the spirit of the mind becomes the new Ark of the Covenant, housing the commandments of God. "God is a Spirit" (John 4:24), and his words have purposed "that the righteousness of the law might be fulfilled in us, who walk not after the flesh, but after the Spirit" (Romans 8:4).

11. Let your devotional conversation embrace the sacred calling to become a habitation of the Bible's words and character through the Spirit (Ephesians 2:22). The commandments are not chains, but keys. They are the inscription upon the heart, "written with the Spirit of the living God" (2 Corinthians 3:3), and those who treasure them will find within their souls "a well of water springing up into everlasting life" (John 4:14).

18

Renewed In Knowledge

1. To live a life reshaped by the Bible, your devotional mind must be renewed, reflecting its goodness (Ephesians 4:23; Colossians 3:10). This isn't a shallow change but a deep transformation, crafting a new self that mirrors the image of its character, rooted in wellness and truth (Ephesians 4:24). The journey begins with understanding, and it acting as a light that guides your thoughts to align with the Bible's higher learning.

2. Who forms this new self? It is the Bible's words, uniting what was once divided and bringing contentment through wholeness (Ephesians 2:13,15). Through its philosophy, the living God births *us* anew, making our conversation a cherished creation (James 1:18). We are called to reflect what we learn from the scriptures, which disposition, due to our experience with cultivating a useful devotional character, shines (Colossians 1:15; Hebrews 1:3), following the path of the living God's chief apostle to share in the resurrection of his ministry to possess his passion (Romans 8:29).

3. How do we grow into this likeness? We embrace the will and spiritual wisdom at the center of the scriptures. This will is the law of our faith's regeneration, offering peace to conversation's embracing it (Colossians 1:9; Romans 7:14, 8:6). This wisdom nourishes our inward person, strengthening us to honor what we learn from the Bible with joy (Romans 7:22). Our natural self is and will always be present first, but we must quiet it to receive what perfects both body and mind, staying steadfast in trusting the our experience with the Bible's words (1 Corinthians 15:46; John 6:29).

4. Faith alone isn't enough; the Bible invites us to know it through learning. We're called to serve with passion, as faith is just the beginning (Romans 12:11). These words sustain the life of our belief, granting wisdom to overcome the errors within the religious world (Deuteronomy 8:3; 1 John 5:4). Like inscribed tablets, the law of the Bible's wisdom guides us to intelligently live better (Exodus 31:18; Galatians 6:2).

5. This law is written on our heart through an experience with it, aligning us with the *Temple* above (2 Corinthians 3:3; Hebrews 12:22). Understanding the meaning behind the anointing of the God's chief apostle makes us family to one experience, empowering us to maintain reverence for the same will (1 John 5:1; John 1:12). Without knowing this guiding wisdom, we cannot belong to that family, but by trusting the words attached to that understanding, we live through them, keeping their counsel (Romans 8:9; Proverbs 4:4).

6. Knowledge of the sacrifice of the living God's chief apostle renews our faith's heart and mind, shaping it by knowing his purpose (1 John 4:9). The *kingdom* of *God* is power, not just words, embraced through trials with joy (1 Corinthians 4:20; 1 Thessalonians 1:6). This is the present work of creation, in that we are crafting a devotional self

rooted in wellness, reflecting the nature of the Bible's character through its guidance (Isaiah 32:17; Ephesians 4:24). Its words become wisdom when lived out. (John 6:51; 1 John 4:2).

7. The living God's chief apostle is written of as calling his words the true bread; living by *him* means learning the sound of the voice within those words to fulfill the Bible's will in a pleasing way (John 6:48, 57; Philippians 1:27). Embrace the reward given to perfect doers of the Bible's will, which reward is understanding given through perseverance (Hebrews 13:5; Ephesians 5:5; Colossians 1:12). Self-sacrifice aligns us with our faith's example, bringing us to comprehension through discernment (John 3:21).

8. Our devotional conversation is to grow in faith through applied wisdom. Our belief, it should become pure and active, must share in the joy and in the pain of learning. (John 14:6; 1 Peter 4:19). Transformation requires effort; renew your belief's mind and seek wisdom with steady faith (Romans 12:2; James 1:5-6). The understanding gained brings life, and trusting on the Bible's words builds a foundation for right and knowledgeable devotional living (John 6:63).

19

Conversation With Life
And Wisdom

1. To live a life worthy of the *Spirit* within the Bible's words is to align every thought and deed with the character behind those words, to place our conversation under the authority of "the Father of spirits" (1 Peter 4:6, Hebrews 12:9). The Mind who oversees every devotional conversation, the "Father of lights," offers an excellent spirit, radiant with wisdom and understanding, to those who seek understanding from within the Bible's words (Numbers 16:22, James 1:17, Daniel 6:3, 5:14). Knowing this Mind (the character behind the Bible's words) strengthens the reformer, filling them with wisdom as those words take root within (1 John 2:13-14, Luke 2:40). The reformer's task is to dissolve every commandment into their spirit, guided by the "spirit of judgment" and "spirit of burning," regulating their devotional life by the living God's chief apostle's *name* (Isaiah 4:4, 1 John 5:18). Wisdom becomes their shield, a defense against evil, granting life to those who embrace it (Ecclesiastes 7:12, 1 John 5:18).

2. How do we prove the will behind this *name* and its character? By testing it through wisdom, as Scripture declares: "I have proved by wisdom," and, "I have learned by experience" (Romans 12:2, Ecclesiastes 7:23, Genesis 30:27). The Bible calls us to attend to its words, to apply our hearts to understanding, and to let its wisdom shape our minds (Proverbs 5:1, 4:20, 4:1, 2:2). From its mouth flows knowledge, and the just, yielding to its counsel, bring forth wisdom, inwardly and mentally renewed in its *image* (Proverbs 2:6, 10:31, Ephesians 4:23, Colossians 3:10). This is no passive pursuit; reformers must handle the *Word*, proving its truth by faith, declaring, as it pertains to the living God's chief apostle, "Our hands have handled" (1 John 1:1).

3. The living God's chief apostle himself reveals the will within his *name*: that all who see and give effort to know his words will gain everlasting *life* (John 6:40). The reformer, with enlightened eyes, embraces the promises within those words, persuaded by their truth (1 John 1:1, Ephesians 1:18, Hebrews 11:13). Wisdom places the heart in the head, circumcising it by the experience to give life to the conversation's conscience (Romans 14:5, Ecclesiastes 2:14, Romans 2:29, 2 Corinthians 3:6). A sound heart becomes the life of the body of our belief, aligning the conversation's will with the will within the scriptures (Proverbs 14:30). It is through this soundness of heart that we learn how to keep our self's wellbeing. (Proverbs 21:23, Ecclesiastes 6:7, Proverbs 4:13, 4:22).

4. The author writing the book of John tells us that the *Spirit* quickens because it is the source of the life within the body of our belief (Colossians 2:11, John 6:63, Romans 8:10). To know this quickening is to achieve devotional wellness without stumbling back into religious error, sustained by the precepts attached to that quickening (Philippians

3:10, Proverbs 3:23). Without this experience our belief fails; with the Bible's words, its life is manifested in our understanding, and its truth becomes our faith's lifeline (John 15:5, 1 John 1:2, Colossians 1:5). The reformer lives by the wisdom learned from the scriptures, not their own, letting its brightness shape their conversation (1 John 5:13).

5. The Bible's will is our conversation's perfection, uniting us with it and with our selves through living experience (Hebrews 13:21, John 17:22-23). The old ways of religion cannot cleanse the personal or the devotional conscience, but the example of the living God's chief apostle teaches us that, without separating from a fleshed-based religious experience, we will never achieve the Bible's intended experience for our faith (Hebrews 9:9, 9:14). This requires steadfastness and a willingness to suffer the Bible's exhortation to know the intended *eternal life* (Hebrews 13:22, 1 John 5:11). The reformer escapes the religious world's corruption, alive in the Bible's framework, lifted up by the meaning with that man's willing sacrifice (John 3:14, 1 Corinthians 15:22. Our faith must know that it cannot work for goodness, but rather that it must intelligently claim it. (Ecclesiastes 8:8, Hebrews 5:9, 9:12, 9:14,15).

6. Through devotional sanctification, the conversation draws near to the Bible's mind with a true heart, cleansed by faith in the knowledge of the allegory related to the living God's chief apostle (1 Peter 1:2, Hebrews 10:22). Obedience is spiritual, not flesh-based, purging the mind of false religious ideologies to perfect simplicity (Romans 8:2, 2 Corinthians 7:1). The heart, once veiled, must be uncovered and purified by the individual; no man, *God*, or institution can or will do this work for you (1 John 3:3). Love grows through the execution of knowledge and counsel (Romans 4:13, Philippians 1:9, 2 John 2:6). The just conversation, perfected

by understanding, lives by faith, free from a conscience of religious or spiritual error (1 Peter 4:6, Hebrews 10:2, 10:38).

7. This faith—the Bible's wisdom—justifies the doer of its character, making their conversation, and only the conversation, *holy* (Romans 2:13, James 1:22, Titus 3:7, Ephesians 1:4). The mind, not the body of belief, is the seat of devotion, stirring the heart to love and to fulfill the intended will at the Bible's core (2 Corinthians 1:12, 1 Peter 3:2, Hebrews 10:24). Should our conversation consistently and sincerely manage that will, it will be sustained (Hebrews 10:23, Jude 1:24, Hebrews 2:10). The *life* (perception) given by wisdom and experience sustains our conversation, perfecting it in the fact of the ministry tied to the Bible's counsel. (2 Peter 2:20, 2 John 1:3).

20

Serving With Reverence
And Godly Fear

1. To possess a conversation that satisfies the Bible's higher learning to maintain in its "fear," a reverence that shapes every word and deed into an offering of devotion. The Bible's *Spirit* (Mind) teaches us this fear, promising mindfulness and goodness to those who guard their belief from evil, their lips from spiritual deceit, and their hearts from religious wickedness (Psalm 34:11-14); this is why it says, "Who is he that will harm you, if ye be followers of that which is good?" (1 Peter 3:13). To live according to God in the spirit is to follow the way of experience, a path marked by reverence that prolongs the days of our faith's intellect and encourages peace (1 Peter 4:6, Psalm 32:8, Proverbs 10:27). Wisdom, born of this fear, becomes the reformers guide, ensuring a conversation rooted in the heart's obedience to the Bible's counsel (Proverbs 3:1, Job 28:28).

2. The "fear" of the Bible's living Mind anchors the soul, bringing mental and moral stability to govern the body of the belief (Romans 2:29). The reformer is therefore called

to "sanctify the Lord God in your hearts," and to "serve God acceptably with reverence and godly fear" (1 Peter 3:15, Hebrews 12:28). True worship flows from proving this wisdom, testing it through diligent obedience to cultivate a good devotional conscience (1 Timothy 1:19, Romans 12:2). The heart, seeking truth, declares, "I applied mine heart to know, and to search, and to seek out wisdom, and the reason of things" (Ecclesiastes 7:25). This pursuit of *peace* aligns the soul with right understanding, ensuring a life (a devotional conversation) holy in all things (Psalm 34:14, 1 Peter 1:15).

3. The body of our belief (what is termed "flesh"), when left to itself, craves control, but the mind, renewed by the Bible's wisdom, must govern (Proverbs 4:22). A heart that longs for the living God seeks the Bible's *life*, correcting hidden religious errors through faith in its rightness (Proverbs 3:2). By digging into its voice, the conversation circumcises its heart, retaining its words to offer truer devotion (Ecclesiastes 7:25). This labor yields peace, a quiet strength born of wisdom that steadies the soul for service (Proverbs 3:2). The pure belief, walking in the law of the Bible's philosophy, sees the living God (not literally but via perception), their conversation shaped by reverence for that philosophy's *voice* (Psalm 119:1, Matthew 5:8). The grace given from that perception is sufficient for providing a satisfactory experience with the Bible, continually birthing the conversation anew through faith (2 Corinthians 12:9, 1 John 5:1, Ephesians 1:19).

4. The state of our heart is revealed by the confession of our conversation's behavior, for "in the lips of him that hath understanding wisdom is found" (Proverbs 10:13). A wise heart receives principles to live by, reframing speech to uplift (Psalm 34:13, Proverbs 10:8, 10:19). The just conversation, guided by wisdom, enriches through their words (Proverbs

10:20, Psalm 32:2). These members of our faith's body—tongue, lips, and heart—must be re-educated. (Colossians 2:11, Galatians 5:19). The reformer's mouth becomes a "sharp sword," wielding health to hearts encountering them (Isaiah 49:2, Ephesians 6:17, Hebrews 4:12).

5. Without an experience in the Bible's words, the heart cannot claim, "The LORD was my stay" (Psalm 18:18). Only its words divide soul and spirit, purifying devotion to reflect its character (Hebrews 4:12, 1 John 5:6). The right conversation, "fearing" its wisdom, is kept by its *eyes*, their love perfected through obedience (Psalm 34:15, Romans 5:5, Psalm 119:15). This "fear" ensures a heart stayed on the experience, guarded in perfect peace (Isaiah 26:3, 1 Peter 3:11). Once ignorant to the law of its philosophy, the conversation awakens to its kindness, reckoning its self dead to religious error and alive to faith's higher learning, free from worldly traditions (Romans 7:9, Titus 3:4, Romans 6:11, Colossians 2:8).

6. The living God preserves the faithful conversation, the brokenhearted devotional conscience seeking wisdom (Psalm 31:23, 34:18). Receiving the Bible's words, they understand its "fear," finding the intended knowledge of the Bible's living Mind (Proverbs 2:1, 2:5). This "fear," inseparable from wisdom, births a good conscience through faith (Acts 10:35). The reformer's conversation, rooted in an experience beyond religious tradition, sees the message of the living God's chief apostle at the right hand above, compelling the body of belief to yield (Philippians 3:20, Colossians 3:1). It is in this experience that the individual learns the human religious policy has no right to govern the perfecting of personal devotion (2 Corinthians 9:7, 8:11).

7. Correct "fear" perfects love towards self and towards the Bible's philosophy (2 John 1:6, 3 John 1:4). This anguish,

embraced for the revelation of truth, fills the hungry mind with a right demeanor, transforming terror into health and sorrow into joy (Matthew 5:6). The purpose of maintaining worship inwardly is to serve the intended devotional experience acceptably, ensuring "fear" (an intelligent reverence) guards against religious error (Hebrews 12:28, Exodus 20:20). Choosing affliction over spiritual negligence, the conversation esteems the reproach of a wise understanding as treasure, that "fear" written in their heart to preserve their self from straying into an unintended devotional experience. (Jeremiah 31:33, 32:40, Romans 14:23, Galatians 3:12).

8. Understanding what the Bible would have the conversation experience, the reformer restricts self to gain inward liberty, which is why we are told that "the knowledge of the holy is understanding" (Proverbs 9:10, Job 28:28). The carnal conversation (the conversation dedicated to religious law and tradition) cannot coexist with the Bible's higher learning; one mind of devotion must govern, and only grace enables the creation of a verified service (Hebrews 12:28). With "fear" in their hearts, the faithful stand in awe, their lives reflecting the peace shaped by counsel, sincerity, and honesty (Psalm 33:8, 1 Timothy 2:2). Through the wisdom of the message embedded within the living God's chief apostle, religious error ceases, and the soul, anchored in reverence, serves with a good conscience, alive to the Bible's intended purpose (Hebrews 13:18, 1 Peter 3:21).

21

The Devotion Of The Wise

1. For our devotional conversation to live wisely, it is to live according to God in the spirit, aligning every facet of its conscience—its behavior, demeanor, and self-management—with the Bible's full advice (1 Peter 4:6). Our conversation, seen by others and by *Unseen Eyes*, marks the reformer as a true doer of the living God's will, not by outward show, but by an inward faith that rests in the law of the living God's benevolence, boasts the will of that benevolence, and approves what is excellent through the will of that benevolence (Romans 2:17,18). The wise conversation, hidden in the allegory behind the ministry of the living God's chief apostle, live by the testimony of that benevolent will, their spirit shaped by its commandments to reflect its praise in all they do.

2. Baptized into the allegory of the living God's chief apostle, the doer is buried with him in death, crucified to the lusts of the religious world; its fleshly (religious) desires, spiritual pride, and sectarian vanity (Galatians 3:26, Romans 7:6, 1 John 2:16). Resurrected with that chief apostle at this

present time, the spirit of our belief's conscience retains a newness of being for the experience at hand. (1 John 4:3, 2:22, Romans 8:11, 7:6). This is the true reformer, whose worship is not tied to the body of their belief but to the character of their mind (Romans 2:29, Hebrews 11:6). The *flesh* (the body of our belief), weakened by its own natural spiritual desires, cannot fulfill the Bible's full will, but the words of the Bible give life, freeing our faith's conscience from human religious traditions (Romans 8:3, 2 Corinthians 3:6).

3. The sacrifice of the living God's chief apostle is an allegory educating on the end of human religious ordinances (Ephesians 2:15). Sin (religious error), rooted in legalistic tradition, was figuratively cursed in his death, redeeming our conversation from slavery to it (1 Corinthians 15:56, Galatians 3:13). Our inherited "vain conversation" must be shed, our minds renewed by understanding to escape the curse given through the philosophy of the religious law (1 Peter 1:18, Ephesians 4:23). Will-worship, a show of devotion through human decrees, is contrary to the devotional intention at the heart of the Hebrew Scriptures (Colossians 2:23). Allowing our devotional conversation to exist without religious law is necessary to break the heart's rebellion against an experience by faith. (1 Peter 4:1, 2 John 2:5). This is why the wise conversation, seeking and maintaining the Bible's character, is made complete, wanting nothing (James 1:4).

4. Grace, the creative substance behind our devotional conversation's newness, floods the overwhelmed belief, enriching it with wisdom (Psalm 143:4, 1 Corinthians 1:5). The Bible's *Mind* teaches and reminds, strengthening the mind to govern the body of belief (John 14:26, Psalm 77:3). Without its presence, the conversation retains no power for wellbeing, but with the Bible's wisdom, the conscience of the conversation becomes the source of wise governance,

shaping an experience that honors both humanity and the law of the philosophy behind its resurrection (Ephesians 1:17). Our belief is to pass from the death of religious tradition to unending life of an intelligent experience; this is how we know the living God creates our conversation. (John 5:24, 1 John 3:14, 4:7).

5. It is written that "love" fulfills the law of Moses, therefore advising us to serve one another (Galatians 5:14, 5:13). But how can we love without first understanding the culture and the meaning of love? Laying down our lives for others begins with surrendering the essence of our belief to the Bible's words word, letting its *Spirit* shape our compassion (1 John 3:16). Clinging to the world's secular and religious goods stifles love, but the Bible's philosophy ignites benevolence (1 John 3:17, 2:16, Romans 7:12). The wise conversation wears mercy, kindness, and humility, embodying the living God's chief apostle's law of service (Colossians 3:12-13, 1 John 4:7). To claim this man's *name* without keeping the commandments of his understanding's service is to lack truth, but love, rooted in a patient doing, marks the "born-again" (1 John 2:4, 5:1).

6. Love begins with the underlying philosophy at the core of the Bible. The heart, prone to failure, struggles to do good, but the faithful conversation fights to exist in truth, laying down its self as did its example (Romans 7:19, 3 John 1:4, Ephesians 5:2). This self-sacrificing love quenches spiritual pride, shedding light on something more relevant that an outward show of religious brightness and favor (1 John 3:16). Speaking fact in love, the wise conversation shows compassion, its charity bearing witness to their experience with right counsel (Ephesians 4:15, 1 Peter 3:8, 3 John 1:6). Their faithful service to brethren and to strangers reveals the living God's chief apostle's *name*, guiding others on a

journey to the same kind of intelligent and gratuitous still-ness (3 John 1:5-6, 1 John 2:29).

7. True charity edifies (3 John 1:6, 1 John 5:17). Sin (religious error), tied to human ordinances, is overcome by a self-love that builds up the devotional conversation, not falsely tears it down (1 Corinthians 15:56, Colossians 2:14, Romans 15:2). The wise reformer travails to see the alleviation of the living God's chief apostle's *name* formed in other conversations, their devotion, rooted in the fact of the Bible's philosophy, transforming them into a testimony of love, reflecting the intended will of the Bible for the good of all.

22

The Beginning Of The Creation Of God

1. To live according to God in the spirit of the mind is to anchor our conversation in the Bible's precepts, not through vain ambition or legalistic religious fervor, but through a deliberate, transformative digestion of its fact (1 Peter 4:6). The living God blesses us with "all spiritual blessings" to know the Bible's complete spiritual wisdom, otherwise known as his "Son." (Ephesians 1:3, 1 Corinthians 5:5). The Bible's wisdom is that "Son" because it mediates our experience with the living God's will for our devotional experience. Outward forms of sanctity, devoid of this wisdom, crumble before it, but a devotional life rooted in its truth grants confidence, and an unashamed spiritual conscience (1 John 2:28). The spirit of the mind, guided by this *Spirit*, then sincerely and humbly reverences the living God in and by the understanding gained, justly and mercifully maintaining self by what is personally acquired. (Micah 6:8).

2. Humility without mercy breeds hypocrisy, but at the throne of grace, we find mercy, which mercy is the wisdom and power of the Bible's counsel (Hebrews 4:16). "God resisteth the proud, and giveth grace to the humble," pouring favor onto the lowly conversation enjoying growth through spending brainpower (1 Peter 5:5, Proverbs 3:34, Colossians 1:8). This grace, which is the Bible's witness to the creative power of its wisdom, empowered the first messengers of the Bible's philosophy to proclaim its ability to *resurrect* with great power (Hebrews 10:29, Acts 4:33). Filled with confidence, they bore its life, for "he that hath the Son hath life," and "the Spirit is life" and revelation (1 John 5:12, Romans 8:10, 1 John 5:6). Without this witness, no one can claim the wellbeing given by the mediation of the Bible's *words*.

3. These words confirm our place in the fact of the Bible's intention, dwelling in those who keep its advice (1 John 3:24). When our actions, without human effort, flow from its *Spirit*, we know its influence abides in our belief, which is why it says, "...henceforth know we no man after the flesh" (2 Corinthians 5:16). Like Paul, called by grace from the womb of his traditional religion, we are to rely on the seal of understanding (Galatians 1:15-16, Ephesians 1:13-14). No human teacher can impart this blessing; the Bible alone educates through faith in its *voice* (1 John 2:27). Without the anointing of this guidance, our conversation remains empty, but sincere humility to gravitate towards the Bible's character confesses our acceptance of its growth within us. (Ephesians 1:13, 1 John 4:2).

4. The mind bearing its testimony is rewritten anew (1 John 5:12). As *life* was breathed into *Adam*, so the Bible's words are to breathe life into our faith's bodies, transforming our conversation to reflect its will, the living God's chief apostle being our prime example (Genesis 2:7, 1 Corinthians

15:45, 1 Peter 3:18). This breath of understanding is the reality behind the Bible's manner of creation, which reality is "the faithful and true witness, the beginning of the creation of God" (Revelation 3:14, Titus 3:5). In this experience, old devotional *things* pass away; the devotional experience becomes entirely new, ruled by the Bible's wisdom and philosophy of life (2 Corinthians 5:17, Hebrews 12:9).

5. Having the Bible's wisdom means possessing its life-giving principles imparted to our heart and mind for creation (1 John 5:12, John 14:11, 12:50). Sowing to its *Spirit* reaps an unending devotional experience (*eternal life*), for "the Spirit is life because of righteousness" (Galatians 6:8, Romans 8:10). This "life," which is the light of conversations, is sown for the conversation willing to experiment with it (John 1:4, Psalm 97:11, 1 John 1:5). "Eternal life" is possessing a devotional conversation endlessly knowing the nature of the Bible's character, maintaining a knowledge that transforms the conscience to fulfill the will of that character (John 17:3, 1 John 2:29). The reformer, guided by this *light*, lives by its anointing without fault; this is what a perfectly reformed devotional conversation looks like (1 John 2:8, 2:27).

6. To claim this experience, the devotional conversation must experiment with and keep the Bible's principles; this is the process of sanctification, which only occurs to the devotional conversation (Matthew 19:17, 2 Thessalonians 2:13). How can one experiment with and keep the Bible's principles? Following the Bible's wisdom brings clarity to the conversation and helps its values feel meaningful. (Acts 10:44, 15:8, Romans 7:12). No conversation can perceive the Bible's character without being spiritually reborn through understanding; herein we are shown the will for our devotional experience and are filled with wisdom (John 3:5; Acts 22:14; Colossians 1:9).

7. Wisdom, gained through faith, keeps the heart pure, guarding the body of one's belief from *trouble* (John 3:6). Without the influence of the Bible's character, the conversation's heart remains dead, but suffering for its fact, as naturally as the heart beats, brings newness of mind (2 Corinthians 12:18). Revering the Bible's internal *voice* perfects the conversation, focusing the soul on knowing its will (Ephesians 4:24). This wisdom, being the beginning of the intended creation, rightly forms our belief (Job 33:4, Revelation 3:14, Psalm 119:86). Without this regeneration, no one receives the gifts given through the Bible's essence (James 1:7).

8. Grace, administered by understanding, enables us to serve the character of the Bible with reverence and godly fear (Hebrews 12:28, 10:29). This understanding bears witness with our devotional intellect, breathing wisdom for a healthy conscience (Romans 8:16, 1 John 5:6, 1 Timothy 6:13). Having the Son (the chief philosophy of the Bible) frees us from religious error; this is our faith's law of life delivering our conversation from *sin* and *death* (Romans 8:1-2, 1 John 5:12). The reformer then mentally delights in honoring the law or principle of the Bible's philosophy (Romans 7:22, 3:22, Philippians 3:9). It is through this principle that our conversation is created for a service bearing witness of its positive experience (Titus 2:14, Ephesians 4:24, 5:9). Joined to the Bible's precepts, our faith lives free, zealous for its will, our conversation a testimony of its life-giving *Spirit* (John 8:36, Romans 8:2).

23

The Spirit Of The New Creature

1. To glorify the Bible's living *Mind* in the body and spirit of our devotional conversation is to consecrate both as its own, for our bodies of belief are the temple of its essence (1 Corinthians 6:19-20). Religious error (sin) must not reign in our conversation's conscience, nor should the members of our faith serve a false experience; instead, we are to offer our body of belief as a living sacrifice (Romans 6:12-13, 12:1). This is our reasonable service that adds blessing to the individual conversation faithfully applying the Bible's words. (Psalm 112:1, Revelation 19:7).

2. The fear of the living God, a wholehearted reverence, quickens the conversation, filling its body and mind with right understanding (Acts 10:35, John 6:63). This "fear" overcomes the "body of sin" (or the natural devotional conversation) governed by the philosophy of the religious law, transforming the mind to delight in the Bible's philosophy (Romans 6:6, 7:25, 7:22). We are promised, "I will give them one heart, and one way, that they may fear me," this "fear" engraved within our belief's hearts to keep it steadfast

(Jeremiah 32:39-40). We will naturally cause harm to our *bodies* when straying from this reverence, but seeing as how such reverence is the first step to pure devotional wisdom (Jeremiah 32:33-34, Proverbs 12:1, Psalm 111:10), loving the Bible's instruction brings wisdom.

3. Our faith's body must understand what spiritual negligence prevents its growth and development (1 Corinthians 6:15, Jeremiah 32:34). To be buried with the living God's chief apostle means that our belief has passed away from religious error (Romans 6:4, Psalm 68:20). If the spirit of his devotional character rests in our body of understanding, error loses dominion, making us an habitation for the Bible's *Mind* (Romans 8:10, 6:14, Galatians 5:18, Ephesians 2:22). This *Mind*, when allowed to learn from it, washes away unjust religious desires, enabling acceptable spiritual sacrifices (Ephesians 2:3, 1 Peter 2:5). Like Esther's unalterable decree sealed in the king's name, the Bible's *name* is sealed in our belief's character through its intellect, quickening our natural devotional conversation into the intended healing experience (Esther 8:8, Romans 8:11, 8:13, Colossians 2:11).

4. Because "the Spirit is life" (Romans 8:10, 12:1), every sacrifice for understanding will add strength to it. Freed from former religious error, we embody the allegory of the living God's chief apostle's resurrection, quickened as he was by the Spirit (Romans 5:12, 6:5, 1 Peter 3:18, 1 Corinthians 15:45). Born of the Bible's *Mind*, our faith becomes mental, our inward members servants to a belief fully washed by words (John 3:6, Romans 6:19, Ephesians 5:26). Now sanctified, our conversation hears, listens, and does what is true, replacing fleshly religious vices with virtues of faithfulness, humility, and godliness towards the scriptures (1 Peter 1:2, 1:22, Galatians 5:19-20). The presence of this newfound devotional

confidence confirms the Bible's character dwelling in our faith, bearing fruit in due season (1 John 3:24, Ephesians 5:9).

5. The more our faith grows acquainted with the Bible's character, the more that character is written within our hearts, creating us both personally and devotionally anew (Jeremiah 31:33, 32:39-40, Ephesians 4:24). Our conversation, rooted in the Bible's philosophical culture, reflects its power through the educating *Spirit* attached to it (Philippians 3:20, 1 Peter 1:5, Ephesians 1:13-14). The ever-present ministry of the living God's chief apostle brings us to this educating *Mind*, the grace of that ministry sustaining our spirit (1 Peter 3:22, Galatians 6:18, 2 Corinthians 3:6).

6. In the shadow of the Bible's character lies life; its favor is like life-giving rain (Proverbs 16:15, Hebrews 7:2). Its grace, a cloud of blessing, showers spiritual riches on conversations learning from it (Ephesians 1:7, 1:18, Esther 2:17). It is from this higher learning that our body of belief is to become a new and living creature. The wisdom retained from the Bible doctrine, dropping as rain upon the ground of our understanding, nourishes our inward person, aligning us with its eternal purpose through the law of its counsel (Deuteronomy 32:2, Proverbs 4:2, 1 Timothy 6:3, Romans 8:2, Ephesians 3:11).

7. The new devotional creature, formed by an exercised faith on the Bible's words, knows the Bible and the *Mind* at its core as Creator (Colossians 1:9). Saved by its *life*, renewed by its *Spirit*, our belief receives grace upon grace, our conversation a testament to its sanctifying power (Romans 5:10, Titus 3:5, John 1:16). It is in this sense that, after having passed through the Bible's higher learning, that our devotional conversation receives perfection to life as a new creature zealous for what is right, true, and edifying (Colossians 2:9, Ephesians 5:9).

24

The Security Behind A Refined Diet

1. Joseph's journey, sold into Egypt and placed as overseer in Potiphar's house, reveals a deep spiritual lesson (Genesis 39:1, 39:4). The "wife" of Potiphar, casting her eyes upon Joseph, symbolizes a church, as Scripture likens a wife to the church loved by *Christ* (Genesis 39:7, Ephesians 5:25). Potiphar, a high-ranking Egyptian officer, represents the state (the government), while Joseph embodies the living philosophy of the scriptures, faithful to its principles amid a foreign system (Genesis 39:1). Initially, Joseph served in peace, his integrity blessing the Egyptian *house*, for "the LORD blessed the Egyptian's house for Joseph's sake" (Genesis 39:5). This harmony prevailed as long as the church and state remained distinct, allowing Joseph to honor his God without conflict.

2. Yet, when Potiphar's *wife* sought to seduce Joseph, urging, "Lie with me," the state-church amalgamation emerged, threatening his fidelity to his God (Genesis 39:7-9). Joseph's refusal; "How then can I do this great wickedness, and sin against God?"; sets a sure standard for Bible-trained

conversations to resist the unholy union of religion and state (Genesis 39:9, 1 John 3:10). Fleeing her grasp, leaving his garment behind, Joseph preserved his personal and devotional purity, rejecting a "strange woman" of false or foreign practice (Genesis 39:12, Proverbs 7:5). This narrative foreshadows the historical tragedy of the Papacy, where a church, claiming *God's* name, merged with the Roman state, moving many to worship "the dragon which gave power unto the beast" (Revelation 13:2-4, 13:7). This union birthed religious and political confusion; we should know that "God is not the author of confusion" (Isaiah 14:12-13, 1 Corinthians 14:33).

3. The Papacy (a religious institution), seated on its government or beast (Rome), wielded civil power, declaring resistance to its authority as resistance to *God* (Revelation 17:3, Romans 13:2). This led to a dark age of spiritual oppression, where liberty vanished under the guise of *divine* ordinance (Leviticus 18:23). Joseph's steadfastness, rooted in his God's law, mirrors the call for remnant conversations to resist such allegorical apostasy. The Papacy found itself in such a torrid condition due to its priests, seeing their government as a tool for spiritual ascension, having a political agenda for the supremacy of their religion (Acts 15:5, Galatians 2:4, Jude 1:4). There were none in this age that were like Joseph, who stood firm and remembered the living God, refusing to bow to the beast's *image* (Revelation 12:17, 14:9-10).

4. When the state, symbolized by Potiphar, defends its "wife," wrath is kindled, as seen in Joseph's imprisonment and the dragon's war against the remnant that keep *God's* commandments (Genesis 39:20, Revelation 12:17). Legislation will arise to protect the false church, punishing those who honor the Bible's voice over human religious decrees, yet the faithful will say, "Whether it be right in the sight of

God to hearken unto you more than unto God, judge ye" (Acts 4:19). This resistance, grounded in intimate communion with the Bible's philosophy, guards against deception (1 John 4:1, 2 Peter 2:3).

5. The security behind this stand lies in a refined spiritual diet, binding the Bible's character to the heart as "the apple of thine eye" (Proverbs 7:2-4). Joseph's temperance, fortified by the "sword of the Spirit," enabled him to flee temptation (1 Corinthians 9:25, Ephesians 6:17). Similarly, our belief must cultivate a disciplined conversation, executing the Bible's principles to regulate its mind and body (Philippians 1:27, 1 Peter 1:22). This diet, refined through obedience to what one retains from personally studying the scriptures, rejects fleshly spiritual negligence, writing the law of the Bible's counsel on the heart to produce a new devotional creature (Ephesians 4:24, Titus 1:1).

6. As a new religious republic emerges, being "another beast" with lamb-like horns, it will deceive with claims of universal *holiness*, proclaiming, "All the congregation are holy" (Revelation 13:11, Numbers 16:3, Psalm 82:6). This false system, born from spiritual upheaval, will push denominations to its agenda, robbing the *home* of the Bible's wisdom of its garment (Deuteronomy 33:17, Zephaniah 2:2). Yet, the faithful, having wrought the peace of understanding through obedience, will stand uncompromised, their behavior reflecting the patience of the Bible's impression (Zephaniah 2:3, Titus 2:3). Like those Hebrews in Babylon, who yielded their bodies to serve only their God, they will face fury but emerge unharmed, the honor of reverencing the Bible's counsel preserving them as intended (Daniel 3:19, 3:28, Jeremiah 27:8).

7. This refined diet, completed in quiet seasons of fellowship with the Bible, equips conversations for the coming

trial of their faith (Philippians 2:1, 2:12). By working out salvation with fear and trembling, the soul is sealed against betrayal, rooted in an intellect that transforms the conversation into a secure habitation (Ephesians 4:24, 1 Corinthians 7:34). Thus, the remnant conversations to come, sober and temperate, stand secure, their integrity a shield against the *strange woman's* (an unjust theocratic institution) spiritual flattery, ready to glorify their Father in body and spirit (Titus 1:8, Proverbs 7:5).